Terror In Mexico:

The Kidnapping of Ken Krusensterna

Terror in Mexico: The Kidnapping of Ken Krusensterna

By

Ken Krusensterna

Dedicated to my loving family, and
to all those victims and their
families terrorized by random
acts of violence when traveling
on foreign soil.

ACKNOWLEDGMENTS

A special thanks goes to my wife, Corrine Krusensterna, for her patience and understanding during the development of this book—qualities only rivaled by her determination and persistence in her pursuit of my escape and encouragement during my recovery. It is unimaginable for me to think of how my life would have ended up without her lifelong companionship and tough belief in my capabilities.

I thank my children, Keith Krusensterna, Beth Jones and Deanne Krusensterna for their continued positive support and encouragement during this ordeal. It was the power of their memory that gave me the strength to survive when my body and spirit would have given up the battle. Thanks kids for the unconditional love you've given me all these years—it was invaluable during those dark days.

How could I forget all my friends and associates in Mexico? My appreciation for their continued friendship and assistance in the research of this project extends to them all, with a special thanks to Otillio Montoya for his patience and "fill-in-the-gap" details. It was those details that helped our writers get the full picture of what went on in Mexico outside the tiny walls of my kidnappers' hideaway. Thanks Otillio for being my eyes and ears while I was blinded with my own fears and incapacitated by the trauma.

Acknowledgments

I would also like to take this opportunity to share my family's and my own appreciation of the heroic efforts of the local and national government officials, as well of the local police department and participating FBI agents. I believe it was because of their expertise and highly specialized training and experience that I lived to share this incredible story.

Thanks also go to those at Published & Professional Ghost Writers, to include Debi Siegel and Donna Matthews for researching and ghost writing the experience, and for encouraging me to give details to the story when reliving it was almost overwhelming for all of us. Thanks to Doug Siegel for his thorough layout and design and his creative cover ideas. And, thanks to Carol Rennen for her editing expertise, double checking the accuracy and consistency of our story.

Lastly, an ongoing appreciation to all those families who have continued to share or plan to share their stories of pain and suffering so that our next project will have the same life and intensity as this one.

Table of Contents

Introduction

This book is about moments—moments that can alter one's life forever, moments that form one's character and crystallize the importance of one's existence. Throughout its pages, this book illustrates the fact that it only takes one moment, one experience to change the rest of your life. Rarely has any work made that point more poignantly clear. Within these pages you'll see an incredible story unfold and a changed man rise from the rubble. Along the way, you may discover, as he did, that one is defined by his or her inner strength wherein resides a spirit so strong that it reigns supreme despite being kidnapped, shot, repeatedly beaten and tortured, starved and stripped of all apparent dignity. You may just discover that what you do and say is really not who you are at all, but, rather, you are what you believe yourself capable of becoming. By that one discovery, one epiphany, one moment in time, YOUR life can be changed forever as well!

Should you choose to come with us on this soul-searching journey, we cannot promise you fun-filled reading or light entertainment; that is not the author's objective. His goal, rather, is to create better awareness of the dangers of traveling into Mexico and the knowledge that this is no isolated incident—it could happen to you. However, there is a greater purpose, another goal of the author's, which is not so obvious. It is his goal to encourage you to look within yourself and question your beliefs and how those beliefs would dictate your behavior if faced with a life-threatening crisis. Once you come to a clearer understanding of what you believe yourself capable of becoming, you can become that person within you whose existence is marked by greatness. With the overwhelming power and confidence offered by unwavering belief in what you can accomplish, you can discover life's purpose and fulfill your destiny. That's the book's true, underlying objective—to persuade you to place yourself within the tortured mind of the captive and create within you the opportunity to experience a personal epiphany that holds the potential of life-altering insight.

Not all readers will respond to the underlying message held within these pages, nor will they choose to make those life-altering discoveries and pursue their destinies. For them, this work will be just another book about someone else's experiences. They will continue to observe the game of life from the bleachers rather than participate in that 60-yard, game-winning touchdown or that 60-second, gold-winning Olympic vault. For those readers, this book holds nothing more than entertainment value with perhaps the promise of a movie to follow. The author would like you to know that although that's an acceptable reward for your purchase, you are settling for so much less than life has to offer.

In order to get you out of your seats and into the game, this book comes complete with a unique challenge for each one of its readers. You are challenged to truly experience all life has to offer you, personally—its regrets and rewards, its negatives and positives, its setbacks and successes. Don't avoid the negative setbacks in your life and regret they happened to you. Confront them head-on and learn the lessons they were meant to teach. Don't observe life from your dingy; instead, dive into the ocean of life head first, open your eyes to the sting and look at all the beauty of that colorful, unbelievable world lying just below-the-surface. Is there a reef? You bet, but only there can you become one with the most unusual, unique and colorful life. It cannot come to you, and if you simply throw in a line now and then and fish for its existence, you'll either pull up an empty hook or you'll destroy its promise of a life beyond your wildest imagination.

Still don't understand your challenge? Okay, perhaps you prefer to think of it as an assignment. As you read this book, give life to the story being shared by placing yourself in that room, in that chair, with those desperados. Ask yourself—"What will I do? How will I survive this? When I escape, what will I have learned to make me a better person?" Then, the next time you face your own crisis, cherish the experience. Thank those who participate in your struggle for offering this gift of greatness. Without them— without the crisis—you may never have come to realize the strength of your own inner spirit. Finally, once you believe in the power of that inner spirit, spread the news. Make up your mind to do whatever, and I mean whatever, it takes to help yourself and others change from being life's observers to true participants.

In the process you'll live your purpose and fulfill your destiny. Don't be surprised if your destiny is not at all what you imagined it to be. If you're a construction worker, your destiny may lead you on the road to artistic creativity. If you are a secretary, your destiny may place you into the role of corporate leadership. If you are ruled by your intellect, your destiny may reveal the need for faith and acceptance of others far different from your normal circle of friends and acquaintances. Or, you just may discover you are already on your life's path, and in that case you'll receive validation.

Whatever your experience, it is the author's goal that you have one—a personal, unique one that leads you to higher levels of understanding and greater heights of personal achievement. Make a conscious decision to make this book your experience, your moment, your epiphany! Then make it your goal to share those life-altering possibilities with your partner, your children, your parents, your best friend or, for God's sake, your dog, if it's the only one close enough to you to listen. Once you've learned the lesson, it must be shared to be fully appreciated by you and others. The power of this book is not in its reading or in the challenge it presents, and it's not even in your decision to experience its underlying message—the power is in your willingness to ACT on those changed beliefs. Knowledge without action is empty and meaningless.

One last request! Look on the back page for ways to contact the author and then do that. Share with Ken Krusensterna your story, your personal epiphany. Perhaps you'll become a part of his next book. Within its pages, your published story might just allow you to follow your destiny and become the teacher of discovered greatness. I would wish you good luck, but should you accept this challenge, luck will have very little to do with the experiences you're about to encounter. So, I wish you good purpose, strength of spirit, power of precise action and the fulfilling pursuit of your destiny!

CHAPTER ONE
Recollection

For a godforsaken 12 days, I had been held captive, shot, repeatedly beaten, threatened, stripped naked and chained to a raw, wooden chair. I was given no food and little more than one-half a Dixie cup of water each day in the sweltering heat of the Mexican border town of Reynosa. I had heard endless shouting, smelled the sourness of my own body odor and secretions, and felt many times the tip of a gun jammed into my cheek. So this morning when I awoke to the words, "Get that shit out of here! What are you, a moron?" it seemed like just one more morning added to the past 12 that had been dealt to me.

I had been close to delirium for the past few days, but deep down I knew there was something different about the words I had just heard. The woman's threats came again. Only this time, I opened my eyes slightly to find my daughter in a fit of rage at one of the poor hospital aids. I could hardly make out the scene in front of me; and in another time at another place, it may have been somewhat comical. There was my oldest child, Beth, shouting for this Mexican youth to "get a clue!"

Throwing her arm up, Beth knocked a tray of tacos, rice and beans across the room. The food splated against a whitewashed wall then slid to a colorless mound at the feet of the frightened aid who quickly turned to leave. "That's my girl," I thought to myself, somewhat relieved at the familiar scene of Beth having a fit because things didn't go her way. Out of my three children, Beth is the emotionally charged one in the bunch. She runs on about 90 percent passion and 10 percent logic, but that passion could touch a thousand hearts. She is a real Daddy's girl, running in the trucks with me since the inception of my transportation business. In fact, it was Beth who offered to trade places with me during the kidnapping. She was actually willing to subject herself to the horrors of my captives if only they would let me go.

Yeah, it would be Beth who would yell at the hospital staff—eager to protect and defend and never afraid to speak her mind. Whatever Beth feels, she says, sometimes to my embarrassment, but I wouldn't change her for anything in the world. Beth was always kind of a cactus kid—rough and prickly on the outside, but full of life-giving energy on the inside. Sure, she partied too hard during school, but Beth always managed to stay out of the real trouble. As a grown woman, she is happiest controlling a headstrong Arabian horse, so owning her own ranch in Arizona is the perfect setup for her. Yeah, for Beth, life was good—until somebody threatened to take her Daddy from her. A smile crossed my face as I imagined what would have happened to the bad guys if Beth had gotten a hold of 'em!

In the beginning of my awareness, I couldn't quite make out what was going on. However, somewhere through my confusion and the concern showing in my swollen, wrinkled brow, I was able to decipher the jest of what had just happened. Apparently, I was in some sort of hospital, and the dietician had just made the unfortunate choice to send up Mexican food for my first solid meal since being kidnapped and held ransom for two weeks by a Mexican gang. Beth was right to throw such a tantrum. After having been subjected to unimaginable cruelties, I wanted nothing to do with anything Mexican, including their food. And, Beth wasn't having any of it either—she made it clear there was to be no reminders of my past twelve-day ordeal with evil! With that, I allowed the darkness to overtake me again, and I settled in for a short respite.

As I slipped back out of consciousness, my thoughts were not of the fear of being beaten to death or dying at the hands of my assailants, but rather of my family. And, for the first time in weeks, I slept calmly. I was reassured by the fact that she was there—caring for me and not letting anything happen to me while I closed my eyes for just a little while longer. Not even the numerous tubes attached to my body or the weight of the bandages on my head could distract me from falling into the blessed release of sleep. Since the night of the kidnapping, this was the first time I could drop off to sleep without worrying that I would be unable to breathe. I didn't have to taste my own blood in my nose and mouth as I sucked in hard to breathe through my scab-clogged sinuses. I didn't have to shut out the stench of my own urine or ignore the sounds of animalistic sex going on somewhere close to me. And, I didn't have to overcome the numbness caused by being blindfolded and chained to a wooden chair.

"Ken—Sweetie." I thought I heard my name being whispered by Corinne, my wife of 38 years. I flitted my eyes open only to discover I was on the edge of another dream. Corinne was nowhere to be seen in the sterile atmosphere of tubes that I imagined to be the chains that had previously bound me to a chair. Where was the woman I fell in love with as a brass, young colt roaming the green belt of Wisconsin? "Corinne—Corinne," I mumbled in my sleep, worrying that these Mexican devils had captured her as well. Then, as I sunk deeper into my dream-like state, I realized that Corinne would never fall for their shenanigans. Not my Corinne. Her fragile blonde, blue-eyed appearance was only a clever disguise hiding that tough, independent interior. When we met, I realized Corinne was years beyond her chronological age in maturity and common sense, and I had to have her. She was a woman no man could claim; she would refuse to be owned by any man, no matter how successful or persistent. All I could hope for was to use some of that old charm my grandfather had swore we Krusensterna men possessed in great measure.

Every time I would catch a glimpse of her graceful gate as she passed me in town, or hear her confident laughter while she talked to one of her many friends, a part of me became more and more determined to make her mine. That's how I've always been—determined, persistent and, at times, impractical to have what I want. It would take a strong woman to stand up to my pursuits, and Corinne was just the woman. It didn't take me long to realize she was one of those resistant, "convince-me" types. If I wanted her affection, I would have to earn it. But the knowledge that she wasn't going to be an easy conquest drew me to her all the more. Although other women were attracted to my naval uniform, Corinne was immediately turned off by it. In our courtship days, some got the wrong impression of women who dated service guys, and Corinne didn't want her reputation to be questioned for being seen by her friends with me—the sailor.

It took all my patience, a great deal of planned coincidental run ins, and several attempts at the humble approach before Corinne finally agreed to go out with me. Then the inevitable happened. Murphy's Law! As luck would have it, I was late to pick her up for our first date. "God, how could I have let this happen," I berated myself as I approached her front door. But, I was prepared with one hell of a story to excuse my tardiness. I had worked on the story for the past 30 minutes, and she'd just have to buy it. I raised my hand to knock at the door, sucked in a deep breath, drew my shoulders back and prepared for battle. "Sorry Ken," said her roommate. "Corinne left about 20 minutes ago."

"Where did she go?" I questioned, somewhat indignant, having had few women stand me up.

"Well, I believe she said she was going . . ."

My anger blocked out the rest of what was being said as I ran back to my car and headed for the club where we had first met. Mistakenly, I thought I could hunt her down and explain away my rudeness. As I entered the front doors of the club, Corinne was the first one I saw dancing with her friends and having a great time. To my chagrin, she didn't seem upset at all that she'd had to go it alone. The picture she presented was a far cry from the moping woman at home who waited by the silent phone. After a few moments, I slunk up to her and offered her a ride home in order for me to explain the dilemma. Once again, I got the cold shoulder—once again, I was up for the challenge. In the end, I won out, and we dated for two months before we got married. The day she said she would marry me was one of the greatest days of my life, and every day of our marriage she has continued to amaze me with her strength and support, her unconditional love and her tireless patience with me.

My thoughts began surfacing, and my eyelashes lay heavy on my cheeks. Those thoughts of my happy days of courtship with Corinne were over, and reality was setting in. No matter how hard I tried, I couldn't get rid of the incessant chills, the uncontrollable shakes and the need, so foreign to my makeup, to feel safe and secure. During those first few days in the hospital, I felt as weak and vulnerable as a newborn, even though I came packaged as an extra-large, ex-military man. When I opened my eyes again, I realized that my vision of Corinne had been just that— a vision. I glanced at the barren walls and the simple furnishings of the dimly lit room. Then, spanning the room, my gaze settled on Keith, my youngest son.

"Shit, am I dying, and they've called all the family in to pay their last respects?" I tried to call out to Keith, but the rawness of my throat and the weakness of my body caused my lips to ignore the pleadings of my mind. No matter what the case, I was glad to see Keithy, at least one more time. That's what our family members had called Keith since he was knee-high to a grasshopper—Keithy. I never would have guessed that he would hold the keys to freeing me from my chains and play such an important role in my release.

Terror In Mexico:
The Kidnapping of Ken Krusensterna

Twenty-one years old, just graduated from college and, to think, he could handle such a family crisis! I've been told by many that he did a great job juggling the difficult tasks as liaison to a bunch of crazy kidnappers, and I'm really not surprised. Keith's methodical mind and organized thoughts have most always allowed him to keep his emotions in check. I'm quite sure the kidnappers hadn't counted on the tigers they'd grabbed by the tails, and none were prepared for the fight that was about to ensue. These tigers weren't about to just hand over their leader without clawing and biting his way to freedom. I closed my eyes, secure in the knowledge that Keith was there keeping vigil, prowling the night, expecting the unexpected. I could sleep—it was over; or was it?

There was one other member of the family I longed to see—Deanne. Deanne is the typical middle child. She's level headed, responsible, and non-intrusive most of the time. If needed, though, she takes position and fires with the rest of the Krusensterna clan. It was Deanne who held things together on the home front while I was wasting away in that Mexican hell-hole. It was Deanne who made most of the early phone calls and dealt with the invasion of the FBI in our Texas home. She was the calming voice of reason during this storm of emotional upheaval. Deanne is like the backbone of our family, flexible but firm, holding the rest of us together. It was Deanne who saw Corinne through her bout with lung cancer and trauma after the operation. And it was Corinne who endured the possible loss of her husband, the father to her children, and the security those things had always provided for her.

You know, no family should have to endure what I put my family through. Yep, I said it was "I" who had put my family through all this. It's unimportant that these bandits had taken advantage of a man who was ripe for the pickin'; what is significant is that I allowed myself to become a victim. God, I didn't want to think about that then. I wanted to blame the Mexicans; I wanted to blame the government; I wanted to lay the blame anywhere but where it belonged—on me!

Both in my personal and business life, I had made many mistakes and been forgiven many times by my loving family. I believed it was my responsibility to make the decisions and my family's obligation to abide by them. As I look back on it now, I see that I was incredibly selfish during our marriage. Sure, it was easy to be the father when I got home from work, and the kids were so happy to see me that they forgot about all the problems of their day. It was easy to come home to an immaculate home, where Corinne made sure dinner was waiting, and there was a warm welcome for me at the door. Sounds a bit like "Father Knows Best" when I think about it, but that's how my family has always made me feel—like I know best. With the constant threat of business detours and personal roadblocks, it never occurred to me that they could have made my road to success much rockier!

At the time of the kidnapping, my partner and I owned an international trucking company. Like my other endeavors, I worked hard and our posted profits were evidence to that fact. Failure had never been in my vocabulary. If I couldn't make money one way, I'd just look for an alternative route. In the past, I thought of success in terms of our finances, and, lucky for me, Corinne thought of success in terms of our family. We made a great pair, and I'm glad I'm alive to finally thank her and the kids for their dedication to the family.

It was after my stint in the Navy that I first got involved with the trucking industry. I had worked my way up through the ranks of Kimberly Clark to become their National Sales Manager. There, at Kimberly Clark, I got to be "lead dog" and very used to the ever-changing scenery and head-on challenges of leading the company to boast greater profits than ever before. It was a kick knowing I played such a significant part in our team's overall success, and it boosted my confidence to continue to hold onto my own dreams, no matter how far fetched.

We were living in Wisconsin at the time, but my job later caused us to move to Atlanta where we settled into life as well as we could. Atlanta was a beautiful city—very cosmopolitan, but it didn't quite live up to that reputation the South has for hospitality. Corinne was a trooper, though, and worked hard on the home front to be friendly and welcoming to neighbors who rarely spoke to us. In fact, we teased, calling them "waver neighbors." Whenever we'd see a neighbor as we worked in the front yard or brought in groceries through the garage, everybody would wave as though we were great friends, and that was the extent of it. It wasn't really that they were standoffish but merely the fact that few had time to socialize around their busy schedules. So, Corinne stuck close to the family, and that's where she stayed, to the benefit of us all.

It was a rule of hers that our family was our priority. She would have none of this stuff where kids played in so many different sports or activities that they were never at home. Our kids chose one activity, and they gave that their all. With after-school projects somewhat curtailed, they actually had time to study and be productive members of our family. It was a good rule—just one of many Corinne was wise enough to enforce.

I mention this because our family dynamics played such an important role in my safe return. It is because of my family that I am here today to share my story after having been to hell and back. As much as I would like to take credit for being the tough guy and surviving this latest tragedy in my life, I cannot in all honesty do so. It's time I did the right thing and gave the entire Krusensterna clan their due. It wasn't me that saved that day—in reality, it was my stupidity, selfishness and greed that made the entire situation possible, but we'll get into that later. Back to the family.

After Atlanta came Alabama, where we lived for four or five years. I am sure Corinne sees it as a wild hair of mine (and maybe it was—that's the way I work). I decided we would go back up north to build a hotel. We knew nothing of the business, but that's what I had decided we were going to do. I refused to let a simple little thing like having absolutely no experience or skill in hotel management stop me, so off we went!

There, in pursuit of another one of my dreams, we owned 7 ½ acres just a mile from the casino in Wisconsin. What an opportunity to make a financial killing. We took our family and dreams up to Wisconsin and built the hotel and a house at the same time. I've never been known to do things slowly or cautiously, and Corinne and the kids were well aware of that by this time. Because Corinne had made it her career to take care of the home, the hotel business was right up her alley. She took an active role in giving us the most bang for our buck by seeking out great deals on the bedding, furniture, fixtures and everything else we needed to become successful innkeepers.

The hotel was a sight to behold when she got done with it, and we opened just after the new year. It was quite rewarding to see that everybody else thought so too; in fact, we did great on our referral business alone, not to mention on newcomers who dropped in to give our attractive inn a try. Soon our reputation for having a clean, friendly inn spread and our business was booming. People would come by bus to gamble at the casino and stay at the neighboring hotels, including ours. But it wasn't like we didn't have our share of setbacks. When the busing company had a falling out with the Native Americans who owned the casino, we feared our business would suffer. We needn't have worried. By that time, we had enough of a customer base that our rooms continued to be booked weeks in advance.

Just about the time the hotel was going gung ho, we discovered that it stood on a parcel of land that was keeping the tribe from becoming a sovereign nation. No problem—we made it clear that for the right price, we could be bought. Well, supply and demand dictated the land's value, and it didn't take a genius negotiator to determine what the right price was to get us to "leave Dodge" so to speak. I don't know how they did it, but once again the family made the necessary adjustments for my next adventure, and we headed for Texas to a brand new life and brand new company.

As usual, I was pumped for the challenges of a new business, but all this moving and constant adjusting had taken its toll on Corinne. Although we had pretty much arrived at financial independence, Corinne had a new battle to stage—one with a malignant tumor in her lung. She had always been so strong, I automatically assumed she was invincible, and she wasn't about to let me see anything different. She sucked it up and rarely complained at the pain and inconvenience of her illness. They removed her lymph glands and about 1/3 of her lung and managed to "get it all," they thought. I'm sure Corinne has to live with the daily fear of its return, and that's a terrible burden to carry. But she's done it in silence and continues to make her focus her family.

It was appropriate that as I skirted the edge of death in the hospital, I thought of the most important thing to me— my family. So, as I recovered from my 12-day stay in hell, Corinne was battling lung cancer, Deanne was nursing her mother, Beth was managing the hospital staff, and Keith was standing guard in my hospital room. As usual, the family was united; it was the Krusensternas against the rest of the world, and we were making a good showing! Tragedy has a way of making life seem so sweet and a way of making each moment with those you love memorable.

Once more I glanced at Keith as the room darkened, and he settled in for the long night. The strain of these past weeks showed on his young face. He had been asked to carry the Krusensterna torch, but the burden of being head of the household was a lot to ask of a 21-year-old boy. What am I thinking? After all he has been through, Keith has stepped from boyhood to manhood; I am alive because of it. It didn't hit me that night that I was actually untied, free from the stench and disgust of my captives. It would be weeks before I would reflect on just how close to death I had come, months before all my wounds would heal, and a lifetime before the nightmares would end! Herein lies my story!

CHAPTER TWO
Day One

Have you ever had a day that never should have been? Well, it was one of those days for me. It was the typical day before I was to enjoy a pheasant-hunting getaway, and nothing was going right. My excitement over the next day was waning, because I just couldn't seem to be done with this day's shit. Some last-minute meetings were detaining me, but the businessman in me knew that more meetings meant more money, so I had to bite the bullet. I flew from my company headquarters in Dallas, about 500 miles south to Harlingen, Texas, where I planned to drive into McAllen. McAllen is your average Texas border town, and I habitually made it my port of entry into Mexico, Reynosa to be exact.

I got into the office about 8:00 that morning, did some paperwork, and stayed until just before my flight from Dallas to Harlingen. Satisfied that things were running smoothly, I decided not to fly my private plane and took a commercial flight this time. Perhaps it was the idea of feasting on that gigantic bag of peanuts in flight that influenced me to fly commercial, who knows? I may have smirked over the little tidbits they called a snack, but I would have given a king's ransom to have had a bag of peanuts during the 12 days that followed. Thank God I ate the whole bag; I had no idea how long they would have to sustain me.

After landing at the airport, I headed over to pick up my rental car and make a reservation at the Country Suites Inn in McAllen. Getting the rental car was the first in a strange series of events that significantly made it more difficult for the authorities and professional investigators who would later be trying to find me. Usually so precise about calling in when there were any changes to my travel plans, this time I failed to report that the blue Ford Taurus which had been originally assigned to me had now been exchanged for a maroon Taurus. No big deal, I thought, I'll just take the maroon Taurus since the blue one was blocked in its parking space. Not only did I fail to notify anyone of the change, but the rental company failed to make the switch on my registration.

Okay, so what's the big deal? Blue Taurus—maroon Taurus—pink and green Taurus—why make a fuss over a mere little rental car? Well, when push came to shove, and everybody under God's green acre was looking for me, what color car do you think they were searching for on the streets of Reynosa? Blue for God sakes—BLUE! I had broken one of the most important rules a foreign traveler must remember when planning to spend time in Mexico. I had failed to notify my family or somebody at my offices that there had been a change. I had forgotten that even the smallest of changes could mean your life when you're in a crisis! If that had been my one and only mistake of the decade, it may not have mattered much, but it was one at the top of a huge pile of blunders.

My first order of business was to check into my hotel and prepare for a meeting I was to have with a Zenith big-wig. Since I owned a trucking company that transported products back and forth between Mexico and the United States and Zenith manufactured the products that needed transporting, it was logical we could do business together. Zenith was actually only one of several major companies for which we hauled. It was a whole lot more economical to use one of our twenty-five rigs and drivers than it was for these companies to have to go into the trucking business as well as the manufacturing business.

I was in my car, heading toward McAllen when my cell phone rang—picking up that phone was my second big mistake of the day. "*Por favor*, Kenneth. It must be tonight—they make demands for the documents or they be here to shut us down!"

Rosa's voice had an urgency I'd never heard before. "Rosa, I've got to be at a meeting with Zenith! You can't mean to tell me they couldn't wait 'til the morning for these tax papers?" Rosa's nagging faded to the background as the whispering voice within my head sent a warning signal that I know now was dangerous to ignore. I could kick myself for shaking off that intuitive, built-in alarm that was alerting me to imminent dangers, but at the time, I simply replied, "Alright, I'll be there tonight. Meet me at the office in an hour." It was time for me to hang up before my irritation got the better of me.

As if to reassure me that I was doing the right thing, Rosa hung up with, "It for the best, Kenneth. I see you there."

What had started out as a mutually-beneficial business relationship between this 23-year-old Mexican

Terror In Mexico:
The Kidnapping of Ken Krusensterna

beauty and me, had moved itself right up into the "pain in the butt" category. When my attorney in Mexico recommended her as my Mexican business partner, she seemed like the perfect candidate. She was bright, enthusiastic, educated and fairly bi-lingual. Even better, she was willing to be a silent partner; sit back and let us run things. I thought I was being plenty careful by checking out her family background. Her mother was a teacher and her father worked for the city—everything fine there.

Since Mexican law requires all businesses in Mexico to be at least 51 percent owned by Mexican citizens, we needed Rosa as much as she needed us. In exchange for her name on the dotted line of our business transactions, she would receive a company van, housing allotment and additional money each month for the few little extras that made living in a border town more bearable. For a while, I thought that would be enough, but I was soon to discover that there was never enough for Rosa.

I had made this trip from McAllen to Reynosa so many times before, I was driving on automatic mindset. My thoughts went back to my start in Reynosa; the trucking company and the business I'd built with all these corporations bringing goods back and forth between the U.S. and Mexico. It was a lucrative living, and I'd always enjoyed the freedom of owning my own company. I sighed as I reflected on the great number of people whose livelihood was dependent upon the success of my company. I guess this meeting was necessary to satisfy the *officianados* and keep them off my back when it came to paperwork hassles. I had nothing to worry about, however; everything was by the book and above board.

"What a way to ruin a great pheasant-hunting trip," I said out loud in my car to nobody in particular, since I was by myself and I hadn't seen one other traveler for miles now. I was getting even more frustrated with Rosa's continuous demands, but "maybe she was right about this one," I thought, in an attempt to still my inner dialogue. There it was, that warning voice inside my head again. Any more delays before going back to Dallas the next morning, and I may as well forget that trip I had been looking forward to taking.

"Ring . . ." I was jolted from my thoughts as the sound of my cell phone on the seat beside me broke through. "Hello."

"Kenneth, it's Rosa. My house is better for tonight—not at the office."

"Jesus, Rosa!" It was only five more blocks, and my increased irritation was really unfounded. As I look back on it, though, it was more than the inconvenience of it all. There was something prompting me to make this an "in-and-out" trip; it was something more than my meeting with Zenith and my hunting getaway. I couldn't quite put my finger on the feeling, so, again, I blew it off. "What's wrong with the office, Rosa?"

"It's my car—she will not start for me. The battery, she is dead. I really am needing you to come to my home," she replied in her broken English, but her response was just a little too tense, like something very important was hanging in the balance.

"Okay, I'm almost there."

"*Gracias, bueno, bueno,*" she said, "I be here." Just before I hung up, she spoke loudly into the phone—"Kenneth, the gates, they will be left open!"

Terror In Mexico:
The Kidnapping of Ken Krusensterna

There was that inner warning again. What the heck was bugging me? Well, for one, Rosa was such a fraidy-cat, she never left the gates open—especially not late at night. "Okay, Ken, this is no mystery novel or Hollywood script," I said, attempting to stay my suspicions.

As I crossed the border, I took in my surroundings. What a contrast—between Reynosa and my home in Dallas. Downtown Reynosa at its best made the barrios in Dallas look good. The impoverished commercial section of town with broken-down car dealerships, grocery stores sporting cracked windows, and half-lighted signs that flickered on and off all night boasted Reynosa's best. Just on the outskirts of town in the residential area, a single dim street light barely enabled me to skirt the potholes and muddy banks. The drive was getting about as rocky as my mood, and if I hadn't been just blocks from Rosa's, I would have headed for home. I turned my head to look out the window. Every narrow street was lined with garage-like shacks with a month's worth of trash piled high enough in front to block the lights of all oncoming traffic. But there was little of that this time of night. I could never get over the isolation and stillness of the streets just outside the city.

"Finally!" I thought to myself as I pulled up in front of Rosa's home. As she had promised, the gates were open but no more welcoming than if they had been locked tight as usual. Her house was nicer and a bit better kept by Reynosa standards; Our company money had obviously elevated her status in life. As I got out of my car to approach the slightly ajar door, the hairs on the back of my neck were tingling, and it was more and more difficult for me to throw off my inner alarm. Later I would regret the ease at which I dismissed those feelings we all have—the feelings meant to make us hesitate in the face of danger!

Nothing could be heard but the crunch of my hard shoes on the gravel drive. My nostrils were assailed by the instant sourness of old garbage and urine. Those are the trademark scents of many border towns in Mexico. In too much of a hurry to grab anything but my briefcase with one hand, I felt it slap against my leg as I reached to knock on the cracked door with the other. I knocked—no answer. I called, "Rosa . . . hello! Hello, Rosa, it's Ken!"

I pushed the door open and stuck my head in when suddenly all hell broke loose! Two men jumped up from the interior and grabbed me—another hit me from behind. The two men inside were wearing ski masks, but their faceless appearances were not nearly as frightening as the long, shiny blade and pistol they brandished. The fierce one wielding the gun stuck it in my face in order to subdue me. Ironically, I suddenly decided to listen to that voice—There was no way to ignore the danger, and I was fighting for my life.

I managed to slug the man holding the gun; I heard the crack as the gun flew from his hand, hit the ceramic tile and slid across the room. Both men wrestled me to the ground, but I was determined they would have to put up as much of a struggle to kill me as I would to be free. The two smaller men I wrestled were over-shadowed by my six-foot, 200-pound frame. I'd like to think I would have stood a chance if it had been just the two of them, but their "homey's" came to the rescue and all joined in the sport of beating me to a pulp.

Terror In Mexico:
The Kidnapping of Ken Krusensterna

Just after I buried my fist in the stomach of another gunman, a shot rang out. My head flew back sideways, and I remember gazing at the blood-splattered wall, wondering who had been shot—never dreaming it was me. I fell to the floor, got up, fell again, got up, and repeated the motion until my body refused to respond. I then fell hard against the grimy floor. What seemed like an eternity since I had carried my briefcase through the door, had, in reality, been no more than three or four minutes.

With my feet and hands hog-tied behind my back, blood running down the side of my head, and my face beaten into an ugly mask of my usual self, I didn't think it could get much worse. I was wrong about that, too. The blindfold was next and then, worst of all, the filthy gag they put in my mouth that made me heave and swallow a mixture of bile that rose from my stomach and blood running down from my nose. Fearing I would choke to death, it took all my concentration to keep from throwing up. My inner voice that had warned me before, was now offering the simplest of instructions like "Breathe! Don't pass out!" But, with a nose full of blood, my breathing was impaired, and I passed out.

It was obvious they had other plans for me besides death; one noticed my difficulties and took the gag off my mouth. He got close enough to my face for me to smell his sweat-soaked clothing and foul breath. I rolled my eyes to the side as he stuck the gun up to my mouth, whispering "sshhh, boooom!" I understood that language—"Open your mouth and you're a dead man!" I had just a few minutes reprieve from the gag before they shoved it back in my mouth and left me there, alone.

It's amazing how other senses compensate when you cannot depend on your sight. I sensed the presence of another in the room. He began spraying this horrible deodorizer around that made me gag even more than the filthy cloth in my mouth. The door creaked open, and I could hear some jabbering in the hallway. Suddenly Rosa was thrown against me. I was listening to that inner voice, big time, now, and I knew this rough stuff with Rosa was an attempt to convince me that she, too, was a victim. In a quivering, yet controlled voice, she began to speak to me.

"They have taken me too, Kenneth," she sniveled. "They got my mama; they say they want money—lots of *dólares*." She stopped, as an actress would pause, to give power to a scene. "Kenneth, they know where your *familia* is."

Of everything that had happened in the last thirty minutes, those words frightened me most. Although I was quiet on the outside, on the inside I raged at the thought of what I would do to them if one of the vultures so much as touched a hair on the head of just one member of my family. As if attracted to the smell of blood, the pack swarmed around me, peeled the ring from my swollen finger and stuck their paws in my pockets for my wallet. The thousand dollars in cash and my credit cards must have looked like Christmas to them.

"Say nothing or they shoot you, Ken," Rosa continued in her sobbing voice. Knowing I spoke no Spanish, the next words from her mouth confirmed my suspicions. One word I did understand her say was *"ciete,"* which means "shut up," and Rosa said it with authority more than once to the men in the room. "Right—convince me now that you aren't in cahoots with these desperados," I thought to myself. Why else would a hundred pound, bound woman have the nerve to order the leader around in a strong voice, saying, "*Ciete!*" I knew now that I had been set up. When had she decided that she needed more—no matter what the cost?

I didn't let on that I suspected, and they pretended to snatch her away. I was alone again. Next I heard the motor of a heavy-sounding vehicle pulling up close to the house; the driver slammed it into park but left the engine running. Now a frenzy of commands, and my captors were back in full force. This time, in order to conceal my presence, I was wound up in a giant piece of dirty carpet like a human tootsie roll. It was hot and tight enough to constrict my lungs. They struggled to lift me into the vehicle; my battered body involuntarily flinched at their awkward handling. As close as I could tell, I was being transported in a van. I heard the slide of a van door and the slam of three other doors before pulling away.

Mile after mile, I felt the uneven roads beneath me— carrying me to God only knew where. Like a continuous beating, one bump worse than the next, one hour worse than the next, one thought worse than the next. In my agony, my thoughts went back to my family. They'd be worried sick! I was so predictable since I'd been working down in Mexico. So predictable that when I hadn't called in to touch base, I worried they might come looking for me and get captured as well. Corinne would, no doubt, be pacing the floors already. The girls would be losing it by morning, but Keith—well, Keith was who I worried about the most. The confidence of youth can make you believe that you can conquer the world, so I certainly wouldn't put it past him to take on the invasion of Mexico. "God, keep my family safe," I prayed. "Keep them safe on American soil!" I didn't know what would happen to me, and Corinne would need Keith's strength. I had no idea just how badly I would too.

My rational mind was starting to wane. "I was screaming on the inside, since it was impossible to scream out loud with two tons of dirty carpet scrapping me and that filthy rag in my mouth. I was doing good just to manage breathing—forget about screaming. My thoughts exhausted me. I vacillated between anger and despair. About the time I was ready to thank God that the van stopped, fear set in. I wondered if this was the end of the ride—in more ways than one!

Not much time to think or fear; they were in action again, dragging me from the van to another house. If they were demanding a ransom for my return, perhaps I had a few more hours to figure a way out of this fiasco. If only I could stay calm, be rational. However, trying to calm my inner rage and fears only took my thoughts back to my family and fear of what the future might hold for them. This was not exactly what I had in mind for retirement—Corinne either, I'm sure. She had been so sick—now this!

"Wha . . .," I grumbled as they began stripping off my clothes. I didn't want to let them know how alert I was, so I faked more weakness than I was actually feeling. I think the anger inside was giving me renewed strength. Thinking they were just going to remove my shirt, I was horrified when I realized they had other plans. About the time I was wondering how to fend off one of those animals who might come at me with something else in mind besides a beating, I decided to show them I had some spunk in me yet and wasn't about to be molested without a fight.

Terror In Mexico:
The Kidnapping of Ken Krusensterna

Fortunately, I didn't have to worry about that as they shoved me down into a huge, lawn-type, wooden recliner. The hard, plastic straps they tied me to the chair with were already beginning to cut off my circulation. I worried that if things kept progressing, my mind would be weakened by the pain in my body. Hope sprung eternal; I truly believed that it surely couldn't get much worse than this—but I was mistaken. Not only could it get much worse, but I would be forced to endure it for what seemed like a century.

When they were finished strapping me in, they shoved pencils under my fingertips and gave my hands one last tightening causing continual, excruciating pain. Then they bound my neck back tight to the chair. I couldn't move without choking. My arms and legs felt like lead; Lord knows what they looked like by now. I couldn't tell what I looked like. The blindfold made the hours run together like one endless black blur. I heard someone walking nearby, and I wanted to ask questions, but every sound coming from my mouth solicited a clubbing on the head with a gun and the reminder of "ssshhh, booom!" from one of the kidnappers.

"Kenneth!" Hey, *mijo*, it's me, Rosa."

I could hardly hold myself from giving her a look that would let her know I was aware of her involvement. She wouldn't have seen it anyway with my eyes bandaged, but I'll be damned if I was her "*mijo*," and by now I wanted to be her aggressor and beat the shit out of her. I resisted, though, and was smart enough to play the game.

"Kenneth, they are wanting to know the code for your credit cards."

I played helpless, "Rosa, I don't know what to do. I can't give them pin numbers I don't have. You're closer to these people. Tell them if I don't get a doctor soon, they won't have to worry about the money."

For people wanting to keep a low profile, these kidnappers were sure a loud bunch. Televisions were blaring, and they never seemed to ask a normal question—it was always yelling out orders or demands at one another or at me. My head pounded from the bullet wound, repeated beatings and the noise. Then, I figured if I was going to get out of this alive, I couldn't ignore what was going on around me. I had to be smarter than they were; I had to use them like they were using me. You could bet that if I lived and ever got a hold of one of my assailants, they'd wish they had done me in when they had the chance.

It was next to impossible to focus, but I was determined. "Listen, Ken—listen to the words, to the voices, to the footsteps, the televisions, the outside sounds of traffic." When I was finally able to focus, I could even hear air traffic overhead and distinguish whether the planes were taking off or landing. Commentary during the NFL game usually excited me, but tonight it was soothing and comforting to hear my own language. A welcomed distraction! The team of commentators became my only friends, and I relied on the television to keep my spirits alive that first night.

* * *

Back at home, Corinne's life hadn't been peaches in paradise either. It was her first day back since the surgery, and her doctors had laid down the law to her that she was to warm up to the routine again by working only a half day at a time. Limiting her work schedule was the only promise Corinne had trouble fulfilling. Since it was raining that day, she went to the mall for her walk, calling home to ask Keith if I'd called. "Yep Ma, Dad has called in about four times. Don't worry—he's fine!"

But, for some reason, Corinne did have this nagging uneasiness. I'm convinced God gave this gift to women so they could keep a healthy eye on their loved ones who roam, whether it be for the children or spouses. She pooh-poohed her edginess as foolishness when Keith had reassured her that I'd called in several times already that morning, and she went back to the house to shower and go to work. That first day, there was no need for alarm; I had called Corinne that evening to let her know I had a meeting with Zenith and that I'd be home before going on my hunting trip the next day. The real worry wouldn't hit until the following day!

CHAPTER THREE
Day Two

Corinne hadn't been to the office on a regular basis in quite a while, and, needless to say, things were not in the order she had left them. The place was a mess, and it took all her strength to put things right again. In fact, after straining to keep up physically since her surgery, she just had to give into exhaustion and call it a day. The first time she looked at the clock that second day, it was close to five o'clock, and she was beginning to worry that I hadn't called in yet that afternoon.

There was very little mystery left between Corinne and me; I was pretty predictable with my routine. Corinne began to voice her concern sooner than anyone, because I hadn't driven anyone crazy with my constant phone calls to the office and home. Actually, it was that same predictability that helped to save my life; everyone moved in high gear as soon as Corinne started asking questions of people I normally checked in with to see when my last phone call had been. Every time she asked the question "Has Ken called you this afternoon?" she heard the same response, "No, as a matter of fact, he hasn't!" Then this kind of confused look would cross their face until another task distracted them.

Terror In Mexico:
The Kidnapping of Ken Krusensterna

Finally, Corinne stopped the whole operation as she got this side of hysterical. "God damnit! Doesn't that strike anyone around here as odd? Ken's been calling into this office and home at least five to ten times a day whenever he travels in Mexico, and today the whole day goes by with no phone call! What's the matter with you people that nobody thinks to send up a red flag?"

Corinne has little patience with anything less than complete competence. She came to the conclusion that if you wanted something done right, you just had to do it yourself. That's when she started doing some calling and managed to discover that I had picked up my rental car but had failed to check in to any of my usual hotels the previous evening. That was the start of the nightmare for her. She called Keith and told him what was going on but warned him, "Sit tight Keithy, at least until I can find out some more information as to your dad's whereabouts. I'll let you know tomorrow what is going on."

On the other side of the border, Otillio, my office manager, was also a bit stressed when he didn't hear from me. Otillio is a good man, a competent worker who had been with Zenith before coming to work for us. He is a solid family man, well educated and probably knows more about English than I do; he had taught it at the university in Mexico City at one time. Having a great head for business and a keen second sense, Otillio was wondering why I hadn't called. Knowing some of my habits, Otillio hesitated to blow the alarm yet, but he couldn't put aside the fact that something was amiss. There it was: a broken pattern, missed meetings, prickly feelings on the part of my closest friends and family that something was up, and day two on the horizon with no immediate relief in sight.

* * *

Today was Tuesday. Surely, someone would be out looking for me. Was it really only 24 hours? Was anyone searching for me? It was surprising to discover later that the kidnappers had waited two days before contacting my family just to ensure I would first survive the beatings. Thank God my family didn't wait two days.

At 11:00 a.m. the next morning, when I was supposed to be home, Corinne tried to find comfort by telling herself that perhaps I had just gone golfing in Central Texas like I had mentioned a few nights ago. Deep down she wasn't buying it, so she sent Keith to the airport to see if my plane was there. It was! That route closed, Corinne really began to get scared. She tried both of my cell phones, as did Otillio. I had two phones. One of them worked in the U.S. for my calls to Mexico, but I couldn't use it to call the U.S. from Mexico. So Otillio got me a second phone to use in Mexico. Corinne and Keith tried both cell phones but got no more than my familiar voice-mail message.

As a sequential thinker, Corinne knew the first thing she had to do was retrace my steps. She called the office and started getting phone records and credit card receipts of places I usually frequented when I traveled in Mexico. She called the hotel and was mistakenly told that I had checked out. They were looking at the previous week's report. The rental car company gave her the wrong information on the car, of course, so every avenue only offered inaccurate or inadequate news.

Otillio was already making calls in Reynosa. He was having his secretary call the police and the hospitals to see what kind of trouble I might have gotten myself into. It wasn't outside anyone's imagination that I might have hit a policeman or gotten myself hijacked.

Soon, Corinne had to call in recruits—my children. Her body just collapsed, and she knew she couldn't do this alone. Deanne called work and said she had a family emergency; she'd need some time off. Keith and his friend Larry made plans to head to McAllen that next morning. None of them slept that night, but at least my little posse had started to form. I didn't realize it then, but Keith was about to launch a full-scale investigation in the U.S. and Mexico. Dad was in trouble, and neither fear, his mom's worry or authorities advice were going to keep him out of Mexico.

* * *

Meanwhile, I felt myself going in and out of consciousness as much as the 49ers had gone on and off the field the night before. I was in shock; shaking uncontrollably and battling severe chills, yet I knew the temperatures had been hotter than blazes just the night before when my captors had taken me. I constantly thought of ways to escape. I could hear normal neighborhood sounds outside. I knew if I could somehow stand and walk then squeeze through the door with all this stuff pinning me down, somebody would have to call the authorities about the naked man walking down the street with an old, wooden, lawn recliner strapped to his back. Even as bad as it got, I had to laugh at that picture. Perhaps I could get them to let me use the bathroom and then overtake the "guard."

When you're in the middle of a kidnapping, pain prevents much of a reprieve, and my thoughts were soon clouded by the horrible nerve ends tingling in my arms and legs. It was like a million ants swarming my body and stinging me over and over until I felt like I would explode with the pain. When that subsided a bit, I felt even further despair knowing now that my limbs would never allow me the getaway I had been planning. Next, my beard began to irritate me; it itched and tickled for hours on end. As difficult as it was to focus on coherent thoughts, it sure didn't seem difficult to let all the irritants get through. The need to scratch was so all-consuming, I would risk the clubbing over my head and the choking neck ties just to relieve the itch by rubbing my cheek against my shoulder. Every time I moved, my watchman would stick the gun in my mouth and yell "no move, ssshhh, booom!" Finally I got so mad I yelled out, "Kill me then! Why don't you just kill me!"

Hours went by, and all I was given were a small chunk of banana and half a Dixie cup of water. When I begged for more water, my guard would laughingly stick a bottle in my mouth and say, "tequila!" I wasn't about to drink alcohol; I knew that would be the kiss of death. My stomach churned at the thought of swallowing it, and up came the bile from my insides again. From all the beatings, dropping in and out of consciousness, and the mental abuse, I gradually began to lose my ability to think through things in a completely rational manner. For example, I had no feeling in my right hand; and when I smelled the stickiness of my own blood, I was convinced they had severed my hand to send to my family. I had heard horror stories of such things being done to convince them to cough up the ransom money.

Getting up to use the restroom was unthinkable, so I was forced to relieve myself in the chair. As the afternoon got hotter, the urine and sweat mingled together to eat at the sensitive skin on my inner thighs. The insects collected in mass on my naked body. Was it only that morning, at the crow of the rooster outside, that I awoke to the knowledge that I had survived another night in hell? Was I lucky, or simply postponing the inevitable? All day people walked by, children played outside, dogs barked and life went on as usual—except for my life and that of my family. Few knew or probably even cared about the drama unfolding within the walls of this shack. Would they care when it was too late for me—too late for my family?

It had only been two days, and I still had a lot of life left in me and enough anger to fuel a great argument going on in my head. I spewed venom at anybody I could think of, but the rage was inside. Nobody to hear my hysteria; nobody to care about the unthinkable injustice that was being carried out for the sake of the almighty greenback. I blamed Clinton for his contribution in forcing Mexico's hand, calling their national loan due and payable. Because of this, the fall of the Mexican *pesos* had created devastation throughout the land. I blamed corporate America for exploiting their poor economic situation by working the Mexican people much harder than their American counterparts yet paying them peanuts compared to the high salaries paid in the States. I think I would have even blamed my mother for my predicament if I could have gotten away with it, emotionally. As I said before, the only one I didn't blame was myself—at least not until I was too weary to pretend anymore. That's when I finally admitted the truth about myself, and it wasn't pretty or admirable; that's for sure.

Like most other businessmen traveling in Mexico, I loved the attention given to me because I was an American "hot-shot" businessman. Many of the people I lavishly entertained often dropped my drunken lump at my hotel and talked about my behavior behind my back with disgust and disrespect. As well they should have. I didn't deserve respect. I was too busy acting the typical American—impressed with my own success and financial profits and none too shy about letting others know just what those profits were.

It wasn't unusual for me to go into a club and flash hundred-dollar bills as if they grew from trees. Keep in mind, this was at a time in Mexico when its people worked a week and took home a whopping $2 to $3 dollars. I wasn't brash enough to brag about my accomplishments directly, but I sure didn't mind my associates doing that for me. Sure, I'd act like their praise somewhat embarrassed me, but truth be known, I ate it up hook, line and sinker! Well, since I seemed to be in the middle of some sort of spiritual cleansing, like self-confession would make a whole lot of difference at this point, I decided it was time to ask forgiveness for my many indiscretions—it was one of those blanket pleas.

"God, I'm sorry for all I've done!" I waited to feel a ton better, but nothing. No warm fuzzy feeling, no reassuring

Terror In Mexico:
The Kidnapping of Ken Krusensterna

light from above and no building inner strength in response to having done the right thing. Why? Because I hadn't! I hadn't had a chance yet to be the man I knew I was capable of being or to let my family know how much I wanted to make it up to them all by being the best dad and husband I could possibly be. Would I ever get that chance? I didn't know—but it gave me something to fight for.

If my hands had been untied at that point, I probably would have beaten myself up for my stupidity. I was a foolish, middle-aged man who needed to somehow prove his manhood by carrying on in Mexico like I was some high-profile, corporate big shot. At first it was an adventure, which turned into an easy routine and ended in this—a life-threatening crisis which put my whole family in danger and jeopardized the success of a company I had worked so hard to build. I could certainly tell you now, it wasn't worth it, but at the time I would listen to nobody.

Otillio had tried to tell me that what I was doing could create an explosive situation, but I had chalked it up to his overly cautious nature and "mother-hen" watchfulness. I was having an affair with Mexico, not because her people seduced me or because my wife didn't understand me or even because I was stressed from the pressures of work, but because I wanted to feel the excitement and power of making a "deal" and hitting the big time in the eyes of others. To a man in his fifties, when the toned body doesn't turn the heads of young women anymore, there is something irresistible about having people, CEOs of major corporations, look to you to help them make prosperous businesses in a foreign country, or so I thought.

Now, I might have to pay the ultimate price for my foolish behavior—I could have to pay with my life, or worse yet, the life of one of my children. The depression and guilt had started to hit me so hard, I almost welcomed another beating. In fact, I found myself doing things to encourage it during that second day. I fought and got a slap to the face or a fist to my injured head. At one point, I threw as much of a tantrum as I could with my limited mobility and energy, which instigated one of the men to fire the gun up into the ceiling. Okay, I don't mind telling you, that made me back off and rethink the situation.

The day passed into night, and my hope died a little with the setting of the sun. It's funny, but my inability to see didn't preclude me from sensing nightfall. Although it was somewhat quieter with the excited chatter and yelling ceasing for a few hours while my captors slept, it wasn't an easy time for me. I couldn't sleep for more than perhaps 20 to 30 minutes at a time, so exhaustion threatened my physical stamina and mental well-being now. In my weakened state, I began to fear the craziest things. For example, sometime during that night it became obvious to me that the man appointed as my guardian was having sex with someone in the room. The grunts and panting went on for what seemed like hours. Not only could I hear their animalistic sex, but I could smell it as well. When they became aware that I was awake, they would taunt me by laughing and throwing liquor on me.

The alcohol burned my skin and attracted the relatives of the incessant insects who had banqueted on my body that day. Now it was really a feast, and I could almost feel my body tightening with the toxins being stung into my inner thighs and private parts. As that second night passed, I found myself becoming more and more like one of them. My thoughts focused on how I would torture my captors when I was released. My body smelled as bad as theirs, and I was unable to get away from the smell of myself. My hopes were downtrodden, and my dreams reduced to the rawness of survival. "God, don't let me become one of them—don't let me lose my mind and become a dribbling idiot for the rest of my life, no matter how short that life might be!"

After my confused reasoning came the fear. I worried that they would kill me, then I worried they would only torture me forever and not kill me. I worried they would contact my family, then I worried they wouldn't contact my family. I worried they would take my money, then I worried they would not be given my money. I finally know how Corinne must have felt when she was told she had that dreaded disease "cancer." Had worry become her closest companion as well? How insensitive I had become. "Give me a chance, God! I'll make it up to her!" Suddenly, I felt like I was back there at the club after having been late for our first date. All I wanted was a second chance, but some aren't lucky enough to get one. Would I be one of those people?

CHAPTER FOUR
Day Three

My lips felt as though they were glued shut. My tongue stuck to the roof of my cracked mouth. I could hear little movement in the house, but that faithful rooster outside signaled the break of another endless day. Were my captors gone? Were they sleeping? Had they left me there to rot? Now there was a new fear I could chew on for a while!

Ever so slowly I tried to move. Even the slightest wiggle or change in position would have felt great, but I was tied so tightly that my movements were miniscule. Obviously, my captors didn't think so—the dip of my head to my shoulder to scratch my beard alerted my bodyguard. He was in my face, this time with a menacing whisper, saying, "No move—boom."

"*Agua*," I crooked through my salty, parched lips, wanting to be careful not to ruffle his tail feathers.

"No *agua, señor!*"

"Please," I pleaded with him quietly so as not to wage the wrath of my keeper.

"No *agua!*" he shouted, just before he hit me. It was bad enough getting a fist when I could see it coming and prepare myself for its contact. However, when I was constantly surprised by fists coming at me in every direction; they landed on softened, mushy flesh yielding too far and too deep to enable me to bounce back.

It didn't take a rocket scientist to get the message that my guard wasn't going to be a hospitable host. At this point, I didn't know what was worse, my hunger or my thirst. I think thirst was winning by a neck. Didn't they realize that if they didn't feed me or offer me more to drink, there was a good chance I wasn't going to last much longer? It wasn't a comfort for me to realize that if killing me was their motive, they would have done it long ago. Those thoughts only made me feel like this could go on forever. No, they had gone through elaborate steps to make certain I was alive and well—okay, alive at least! Still, I was fading in and out of consciousness. I lived for the minutes that I could escape in sleep.

When I was awake, I concentrated my efforts on my escape and busied my mind taking assessment of my situation. I repeatedly did my physical workout of going through each body part and trying my best to see if it was still somewhat functional. I knew my kidneys worked. The animals had not let me go to the bathroom for days, so I was forced to nest in my own fluids for the duration.

"Hum . . . wonder if I can still see? I mean, how limited would my movements and sight be if the blindfold and chains were to be removed right now? I didn't want to go with those thoughts; they weakened my need to fight and resist, my resolve to escape and find revenge. My eyes hurt from the hours of forced darkness. If I could only have one moment of sight, see my surroundings and make sure I was still in one piece. To the best of my estimation, there was a door to my right. I could periodically hear the activity going in and out that door during the day.

Soon the two televisions were blaring again. I couldn't stand the loudness of them, and I couldn't understand much of what was being said, even though some of the time it was in English. Now I was really frightened—I was losing all rational thought, unable to comprehend my own language. Focusing on the fear, at least, helped me to feel something other than my mental and physical pain. Then I was given yet another treat. It was no secret that my bodyguard liked his liquor. He drank tequila like it was tea. I became afraid that he might die or pass out, and I would burn in a fire or be buried in a horrific earthquake and become one of those statistics we see on the 11:00-o'clock news back home. Home . . . I was forgetting what the normalcy of home felt like, smelled like, sounded like.

With his continued drunkenness, I became as worried for the health of my guard as I was for myself. Ultimately, if something happened to him—it happened to me! If he were to fall asleep with a cigarette in his hand and the ashes started a fire, I'd be the one to burn. If he died of a heart attack while fucking his whore like a rabbit, I'd be the one to die in this chair with nobody the wiser. About the time these thoughts were creating an alarmed response, my physical needs took over.

I was so thirsty that, again, I tried my luck with asking the guard for a drink. "*Señor*, *agua*, please."

"Shhh . . . boom" and then came the smack to my head.

It's amazing how used to abuse you can become and how blessedly desensitized your body can be as it follows your mind's acceptance. My keeper's obvious anger just couldn't deter my constant pleadings, "Please . . . please!" I coughed, hoping he would worry that I would choke to death on my own sandpapery spit.

"Drink!" he said, laughing. I still refused the tequila, and he went on with his business. Our most cultural conversation was interrupted by the dreaded cook, who came in each morning to administer to the needs of the gang. The smell was horrible; so much grease! Even though I was hungry, I don't believe I could have stomached one mouthful of her cooking. As it turned out, I needn't have worried about hurting the poor dear's feelings; I was never offered one morsel.

As the morning was scorched by the afternoon, more and more people dropped in to see the chained, naked American, I suppose. More noise! More activity! Precious little attention to me. I was convinced that I wasn't going to be able to handle the pain much longer. My legs were screaming at me, and my ass was completely numb. The wood of the chair had started to eat into my skin, causing blistering in the most painful places. My back felt like I had been mining ore for the entire Industrial Revolution. My head was throbbing from the pain of blood loss and the continuous beatings that just kept on coming. What the hell was going on? Why were they doing this to me and what did they want? I knew they wanted money, but how much and why wasn't my family doing anything?

I could hear the traffic outside now that the morning had awakened daily commuters. It was more of an effort than ever to concentrate on everyday sounds, but I had to. I had to concentrate so that I could use the sounds as a point of reference, and keep my weakened mind active and my spirit hopeful. If I was to have any chance at all of escape, it would be because I was alert to just one slip up.

About the time I started to drift, I heard the soft splattering of raindrops against the window and roof. Although it cleaned the air and created for just a moment or two a freshness about the place, it wasn't long before I realized the additional tortures the rain would bring. Mosquitoes! Armies of mosquitoes! If I could free myself, I was sure I could have saddled them and ridden them home. My thoughts drudged up another worry—malaria! They were vampires, lined up in chow lines to suck the life out of me, and I couldn't even slap the little bastards off me.

Under my blindfold something clogged, something festered. The shot, which splattered blood in Rosa's house, had grazed my scalp, leaving about a three-inch trail. It had also filled my nose so when the gag was shoved in my mouth, I struggled for oxygen. Just to give you a first-hand experience, lock yourself inside a brimming port-a-john on a 50-man construction sight, stick your head in the hole and breath deeply! Now, live it for what you fear might be a lifetime!

My mind skipped around continuously from myself to what my family must be experiencing by now. By now they had to be hysterical. It was simply not like me to go nearly three days without making contact with anyone. I wondered who might be looking and what they were doing. I hoped against hope that they were keeping Keith out of Mexico. I knew that once he crossed that border, we'd have a national incident on our hands. Realistically, I could see them grabbing him as well, and my heart broke at the thought of what I may have created. I knew Corinne would sell blood if she had to, to get both of us home!

Back to feeling sorry for myself. Where had I gone wrong? Did I appear vulnerable? Did I talk too much? Did I trust the wrong people? Yes to all three of those questions. Most of all, did I selfishly satisfy my own needs before considering the consequences? Absolutely! "But, God, I'll work hard and do better if you see fit to get me out of this!" I prayed.

I had heard about kidnappings in Mexico—lots of them—but I never thought it would happen to me. Poor Corinne. How was she faring? I knew this would be such a strain on her. I worried about the family, but they also gave me strength. I knew, in the back of my mind, that my family had what it would take to get through this. As long as they remained safe, we would all be together again. Yeah, we would all be together again. That became my new dream.

More activity jolted me back to hell. They seemed to be carrying on about some soccer game being viewed on television. Those damn televisions and their ten different stations. "If I get out of here alive, I'll never turn on another television!" They were driving me crazy and preventing me from making myself heard. To nobody in particular, without knowing whether my guard was out of the room or simply wrapped in the hairy arms of his latest whore, I managed to sputter out "*Agua!*"

"No *agua*," he said. I didn't know whether to be relieved he was still alive and conscious, or disappointed that I would be given no water.

"Please *hombre, agua*!"

"No *agua*," he responded more forcefully, followed by an upper cut to the chin. I hated to ask, despising them even more that I was reduced to begging, but if it meant my life I'd take up residence on the corner with a cup for the damn water. I had no choice; I truly thought I was dying of thirst. At this point, I couldn't make saliva to wet my throat and mouth anymore. I was already dehydrated, and this was just day three of my ordeal. I knew that more talking was likely to get me another beating, but I had to give it my best shot. "What do you want?" I asked, softly, hoping the others were too interested in the game to notice.

"Money!" came the answer.

"Call Otillio," I advised.

"No Otillio!" he shouted at me.

"Otillio can help," I said.

"No Otillio. *Familia*! Money!"

"Otillio can get to my family for money," I said.

"NO!" and he hit me hard this time, harder than before. I saw stars and couldn't focus my thoughts enough to talk for quite some time afterward. I laid back and tried to fantasize about what everyone back home was doing to get me back there in one piece.

* * *

By now, Keith and Larry were on a plane to Harlingen, Texas. Determined to retrace my steps, come hell or high water—and they were closer to hell! They had told Otillio that they were coming, and he agreed to meet them. While Otillio had been having his secretary call hospitals and police stations in Reynosa, he had also had a driver make visits to all those destinations. It took hours of work and their search netted no positive results. Otillio, Keith and Larry agreed to meet in the lobby of the hotel where I had made my reservation to discuss their united efforts.

Once again, they confirmed that I had never showed up there. Keith and Larry had given a picture of me to the local police, so they would have an accurate description, and the three of them decided they would head over to Reynosa. As they were crossing the bridge at the border, Otillio's cell phone interrupted their silence. There was a slight hesitation, and each cut their eyes at the other before Otillio quietly answered fearing the news he might hear. He let out his breath when he heard his secretary's voice then sucked it back when she told him to get to the office right away. Pressing her for details, she informed him there was someone there who knew about my disappearance. That's all it took—they raced for Mexico.

There, Rosa was in all her glory when they walked into the office. She was giving her Academy-Award performance of the poor pawn in the hands of these *banditos*. Her hair was tousled, her clothes messy and her eyes were red and swollen, like one who had been crying for days. Regardless of the tears, everyone in that room doubted her honesty. Keith wanted to give her an Oscar for best performance by a con artist. I've been told she was good but not good enough to pull the wool over the eyes of those who were sharp enough to pick up on every innuendo.

Rosa began speaking to Otillio and then suddenly noticed all the others were standing there. She firmly said she had to speak to him alone, so they went into his office. He indulged her, and the two of them went behind closed doors for a while.

"They have him; they have him," was all she would say at first. Otillio finally got her calmed down.

"Who do they have?"

"They have Ken and my mama."

"Who has them?" asked Otillio.

"I do not know. Some bad men."

"Is Ken alive?" he asked, looking deep into her eyes for the truth.

"*Sí.*"

"Is your mother alive?"

"*Sí.*" Then the story tumbled out. She said that two guys arrived at her door and asked her if she was Rosa. She said yes, and they pushed her into her house and kept her there. Her mother had just arrived from Tampico, about 400 miles away, and they had her in the back room. Rosa said, "I heard my mama yell and then nothing else."

"What happened next?" Otillio asked.

"I heard Ken at the door. He was calling to me, but I . . . I am blindfolded and gagged. I could not answer to him. I heard a fight and Ken was telling the bad men he had money, not to do anything to him. It was quiet for a minute and then the noise started up again. From there, they took them to a car and drove far away, I think!"

"Okay, so we know they have Ken and your mother. What do they want?" Otillio asked, sure it was Ken's money.

"They want *mucho dólares*—$350,000.."

"Why are you here?" he asked her.

Terror In Mexico:
The Kidnapping of Ken Krusensterna

"They were calling you . . . many hours they tried to call you . . . by phone, you know, and it wouldn't go through. They had to send me."

"Have you seen Ken?"

"*Sí*. I helped him drink water. He is very bad . . . very bad shape."

When I heard about this conversation weeks later, I thought to myself, "What bullshit! She didn't anymore help me drink water than tequila man! In fact, for all I know she was the whore he was pumping every hour on the hour in that disgusting room. How could she betray my trust like that? How could she be the concerned friend one moment and the lying whore the next?" Then I stopped myself. What I had to ask myself then was "How could I be the loving husband and father one moment, and then turn around and put my family through this hell the next?"

Otillio's questions continued. "How did they let you go?" He didn't trust her and was just waiting for her to slip up.

"It was horrible for me! They took me out in a car, blindfolded me and drove around for a long time. I was afraid they would kill me. Finally, they stopped and uncovered my face as they pushed me from the car. They told me to go find you." Otillio found a lot of holes in her story, but he was smart enough to know that if he didn't just play along with her, she could report back and I would be dead.

"Is there anything else you can tell me?" he asked her.

"Only that I am very afraid. I do not want my family involved. Also, they said if we contact the police, Ken and Mama are dead!" Otillio advised her to go home and not leave. She agreed, and he went out to tell Keith about the conversation. Keith immediately wondered what kind of idiots would demand that kind of money on a Friday afternoon, too late for banks, and want it on the next Monday? He decided that his only recourse was to return to Dallas and do his best to see what kind of ransom he could come up with. Keith and Larry took Otillio back to the U.S. to pick up his car, and the boys then headed back to Dallas, dreading the information they would be forced to pass on to Corinne.

Keith had the toughest job of all ahead of him. He had to tell his mother that I had been kidnapped. He didn't know how to do it, but he hoped when the time came, he would have the ability to handle it. There was really no right way to tell your mother that her husband had been kidnapped, and there was a good chance he'd be killed—ransom or no ransom.

CHAPTER FIVE
Day Four

Four days by my scientific calculations—you know, the rooster and all. Four days since I had experienced sweet freedom. My sense of smell was now becoming quite acute, and I could smell my watchman before hearing him attempt to use my cellular phone. Based on his language and the volume of his voice, I took it that his intellect was being challenged by the problem of how to operate the contraption.

I had somehow survived another day; although, I was beginning to think death would be a welcomed relief. If it was possible, the pain in my legs and extremities was even worse than yesterday. My skin crawled with the stings of a million, half-sleeping nerve ends. The recliner had gone beyond creating blisters and had now graduated to eating me for breakfast.

On this day they actually gave me a banana and a Dixie cup full of water. I welcomed the two items like they were banquet for a king. So thankful the banana didn't gag me and the cup of water wasn't lost soaking into my lips before running down the raw muscles of my throat, I reveled in the brief relief. It was short-lived though; the food and drink teased me into wanting much more!

Chapter Five:
Day Four

I was hearing the sounds of outside activity again. This time there was a large truck and a loudspeaker going through the neighborhood. "Thank you God! They've come to announce my kidnapping. Somebody's bound to report the strange activities going on in the house next door." Just after those words came to mind, I feared they would move me somewhere else where not a soul would be able to witness the drama. Then I listened even closer to the truck's speaker, and to my disappointment, it wasn't at all pertaining to my kidnapping but rather asking for that day's laborers.

Time for me to become the expert investigator. After all, what else did I have to do with my time? If I were to escape, I'd have to lead the authorities back here to get the bad guys in order to reap the treasures of sweet revenge. That's when I started listening to sounds beyond the sex, television, rooster and some annoying snapping outside this prison of a house. Sure enough, I was near an airport. To me, airports represented freedom. I had flown more in ten years than most people did in a lifetime. Flying was my love, and I had pursued rather ambitious dreams a while back and purchased a plane of my own.

There was nothing like flying your own private plane. The memories of doing so took me to a far off place where the air was brisk and blue, the silence was only interrupted by the rush of unchecked wind cutting through my plane's graceful wings, and the potent thrill of piloting was uppermost in my mind. Those were the days, and yet I often missed the wonders of the moment for the worries of tomorrow. It occurred to me then how much of the great experiences I'd had were overshadowed by the need to rush in the present, wish different things of the past or worry about what I wouldn't be able to do in the future. Even though I knew that the present was all any of us had, I hated my present situation. It couldn't be all that was to be left of my existence. If I could learn from what I was experiencing and pass on those lessons to others—preventing just one more incident like the one I was experiencing—then my suffering would not be in vain.

Still playing detective, I thought back on all the times I had flown into Reynosa airport. I knew from the sounds of the planes, that if I were still in Reynosa, I was either north or east of the airport. I secretly tucked away this small bit of information in order to pull it out later to put away everybody—and I mean EVERYBODY who participated in this fiasco. There was much tucked away up their in my head.

I waited for the cook to come and wasn't disappointed when I heard her footsteps through the room and out to somewhere where she must have vats of grease awaiting her preparations. "Good . . . good!" I congratulated myself. I was getting to know their routine. All the better for me when the time came to make my escape. My elation lasted just long enough for the sickening smell of hot grease to hit my nostrils and make my stomach churn. It was the fourth day without any substantial food, and I feared I would progress from having chills and uncontrollable shakes to the dry heaves.

As I learned to rely more and more on my sense of hearing, I realized that the cook's talents spread far beyond the kitchen. It was she who entertained my guard off and on during the day. Then I heard that snapping outside again. What was that snapping sound? I searched my memory for a clue, but found nothing that I thought suited the sound. "Okay, let that go Ken. Concentrate on the things that will help to get you out of here."

The pain was unbearable now. Maybe it was because I was coming out of shock, I don't know. Everything hurt from my earlobes to my toenails. Things I had never focused on before suddenly decided to make their presence known through tensed and tired nerves that had been confined far too long. At night I would freeze. It wasn't that cold, but between my dehydration and complete nudity, I couldn't keep my body at a constant temperature. Apparently, my guard got tired of watching me, the stupid American, squirm in the chair and then shake so hard I nearly went into seizures every evening. So he began tossing a dirty, scratchy piece of carpet on me. It felt like burlap and offered nothing but discomfort.

At times I felt I was almost delirious. "How will I die?" I thought to myself. Would they take all the money from my family, then just slit my throat or shoot me and leave me in this stink hole to bleed to death? Would anybody around here care? Would they find my decomposed body in the desert years later and fail to identify me because of attacks by wild animals and zealous buzzards? I knew I shouldn't allow my mind to go in that direction, but depression visited the dark corners of my mind more frequently as one day rolled into another, and I couldn't help but give in to an occasional pity party.

I had to actively revive my hope; and believe me, the sheer fact that they kept me blindfolded was reason enough to hope. I kept thinking that if they were really going to kill me, why would it matter whether I saw them and could identify them? Nope! I was certain they didn't want me to see them so that they could let me go without fear of being identified. It was no happy thought, though, as I wondered how much longer I could physically and mentally stand their treatment. And, I thought I was so tough—I must have been soft compared to the many men who had been held as POWs for years after the war. Now I understood how their minds tricked them into insanity in order to escape the horrors of their reality or how they lost all hope and committed suicide, cheating their tormentors from the pleasure of watching them take their last breaths.

"Get away from me," I commanded the dark thoughts. I realized with each passing day that it was imperative I keep my mind working on an escape route. If they would just let me go to the bathroom, and there was only one of the buffoons, I believed I could probably over-power him. Go figure! If I had been rational, I would have realized that any weight at all on my legs would make them buckle out from under me. And, having been tightly blindfolded now for four days, one peak at daylight would have blinded me if I was even able to keep my eyes open for a second or two. But, did I think about those things? No! That would have brought back the depression, and I'd do anything not to go there.

The first thing I must do is get my guard to remove my blindfold. I kept asking to go to the bathroom for that reason alone. I'd already christened myself numerous times those first few days but nothing recently, and that frightened me. I had been given so little water that there wasn't much to run through the old body to make waste. Too late to be concerned about hygiene! Lucky for me, I didn't know the physical obstacles before me; I would never have, for one wasted moment, contemplated an escape. I had no idea what bad shape my body was in and figure now that it was just as well I was spared the reality of it all.

Again, I tried a conversation, "Problem?"

"No money. Problem," came the gruff reply.

"Did you call my family?" I asked.

"Family, no money!"

"I don't understand."

"Family, no money, boom!" I guess he thought if he added the "boom" I'd jump up in a rage, pull out my cellular, call my family and bitch them out for their lack of response. The "boom" added after almost every sentence had lost its effect. I mean, I knew they had guns. I heard them go off every now and then, lodging themselves in the ceiling or a wall somewhere. What I didn't understand was how much they were asking for that my family couldn't raise the money quicker? Not that I was a rich man, but we could have put together something. Again, I asked for the bathroom.

"No!" was the common response, and this time was no different, including the fact that the response was followed by a punishing blow to the head. I tried so hard to loosen my bindings, but with the blindfold on, I couldn't tell when I was being watched. If he saw me move, he would immediately jump up and whap me. At night, Mr. Military, the head kidnapper, would come in and check to see if I had made any headway. Then he would tighten them even more—too much more and I'd be in danger of my hands and feet rotting off.

Terror In Mexico:
The Kidnapping of Ken Krusensterna

The routine of one day seemed to follow the one before it: cooking, sex, television, drinking, noise, more cooking, more sex and more television, followed, of course, by more drinking. I kept my mind as active as possible when I was awake and welcomed any sleep that I could get. At this point, I worried that it really wasn't sleep I was experiencing but long blackouts between beatings and shouting matches. What was my family doing right now? Was my company still holding up? What did the man from Zenith think of my no-show for our meeting? I had a lot to think about and as time went on more and more to worry about.

* * *

By now Keith had returned home with the news. Corinne was holding it together with the help of prescribed drugs; and, under heavy medication, she too blended one day to the next. She allowed herself to stay numb and let Deanne and Keith keep things going. It was the only way, physically, that she could have withstood this ordeal, and when I came to understand this later, I realized that once again her reason had won out over her emotion. To this day, Corinne swears that deep down inside her female intuition told her that I'd be coming home.

Meanwhile, Deanne and Keith knew it was time to call Beth back in Arizona. She was a daddy's girl and had the right to know. They just dreaded doing so, though, knowing that Beth was the most volatile of the three. How should they tell her? Keith knew a close friend of Beth's, Pam, so they got her number. As promised, Pam called Beth and asked what she was doing. She then asked if Beth would mind if she stopped by for a while. Beth said, "What? You don't have to ask permission to come see a friend. Get your ass on over here!" Pam did just that and arrived just as Deanne's call was coming in from Dallas.

"Beth, you know how Dad always travels to Mexico?"

"No . . . no . . . no, Deanne . . . tell me Pam's story isn't true!" Beth started screaming and tossed the phone to Pam. She thought they were trying to tell her that I was dead. Pam got Beth calmed down and soon Jerry, Beth's boyfriend, was home to take over. Deanne warned Beth not to say anything to anyone, but Beth is headstrong and determined. Much later, Beth's comments were, "I wanted to blow the fucking place up. If I couldn't have my daddy, I didn't care if any of them lived!"

Beth was a loose cannon all right—a loose cannon that had to be contained. In no time at all, she had contacted Senator John McCain's office in Arizona, the consulate and who knows who else. I understand her; things weren't moving fast enough. She wanted her dad back home safe and sound. Beth was frantic. The more detached she felt from the situation, the worse she got. Corinne, Deanne and Keith saw no alternative but to get her to their home in Dallas, so they bought her a ticket for that Sunday, hoping all the official offices would be closed on Saturday.

Deanne, Keith and Corinne talked. "Those devils have had your dad for almost a week now. We've got to do something or he's not going to make it!" They saw no other choice but to call in the FBI. All were in agreement. That very day they placed the call. In moments someone called them back and Deanne answered the phone. "Hello?"

Terror In Mexico:
The Kidnapping of Ken Krusensterna

"Yes, did someone there call the FBI because their father has been kidnapped?"

Deanne was quick. She thought it was a trick by the kidnappers to see if she had called in FBI. "No, you must be mistaken," she answered. "My father hasn't been kidnapped."

"Oh, well, my name is Agent Donovan, and we received a call a few minutes ago from this number."

"Okay, you pass." Deanne told him the story and an agent was there that evening. They knew they had to move quickly.

* * *

Back in Mexico, Otillio's life was getting turned upside down as well. He had returned to Reynosa to pick up his wife and go home. He asked his wife if Rosa had said anything else after he left, and she told him that Rosa had just repeated the same old, tired story. Otillio told his secretary that he would be at home waiting for calls if anyone needed him. He was very concerned by not knowing if the kidnapping was some personal vendetta or strictly business. If it were business related, his family might also be in jeopardy. Being Mexican citizens, they might not have the legal resources that Americans have.

He wanted his wife to take their two children and go to his parent's home in Mexico City. With the crime rate having gone up over 100 percent in the past five years in Mexico City, Otillio never thought he'd find himself sending them back there to be safe, but that was his plan. Well, I'm hear to tell you that even the best laid plans have their flaws. Otillio's wife refused to go without him. He told her that they would have to stay elsewhere then, maybe with an uncle in Reynosa. She agreed, and he called his uncle. His entire family moved in on them for the duration of the kidnapping, which was to be another eight more days. Eight more days—it's a good thing I couldn't see into my future, or I would have made sure I didn't have one. Eight days was like an eternity when I had to suffer like this.

About 8:00 that night, Otillio got a call from Rosa again. "I'm running to the store. I'll be gone about fifteen minutes . . . just in case you needed to call me." The phone call made no sense to him until there was another one a few minutes later. She asked him to meet her at the office, but Otillio was too smart for her old tricks. There would be no one there at this hour, and he didn't want to fall under the same fate as I. He trusted her about as far as he could throw her, if that much, so his response was, "You just tell me where you are, and I'll meet you there."

"Please, just meet me at the office, Otillio." He held his ground, and Rosa finally gave in. "Okay, I am by the drug store," she told him.

"I'll be right there." Otillio asked two of his adult male cousins to go in a separate car and keep an eye on things. They left a few minutes before he did and got a great spot from which to view the activities.

"Get in my truck," she said when he arrived.

"No, thank you. We can talk from here." They made awkward small talk for a minute before Otillio said, "What did you call me for, Rosa?"

"Um, did I tell you how they wanted the money?" she asked.

Terror In Mexico:
The Kidnapping of Ken Krusensterna

"No, you didn't."

"They want $100,000 in *pesos*, and the rest in American dollars."

"What else?"

"Um, did they find his car?"

"No Rosa, they didn't." He was getting irritated with her. "What is it that you wanted to say? I know that there must be more."

"I don't know," she answered.

"Rosa, you could have told me all this over the phone. What is it?"

"I just want to make sure that his family doesn't suspect," said Rosa as she ran her nervous fingers through her hair. On the outside it looked like an attempt to appear casual, but her shaking hand belied her tenseness.

Otillio couldn't believe what he was hearing. So, that was it. Ken's life is on the line and this little bitch is concerned about his family holding her accountable for her actions? Although she socialized with him in his business dealings, she wanted more than he was willing to give, and Otillio wondered if that fact angered her enough to get revenge. She had to be the biggest idiot and most despicable low-life in the world. To him, there was a much bigger issue involved—like how was Ken going to get out of this alive.

Weeks later, when I heard about this conversation, I wanted to spew big chunks. The nerve of the wench! Did she think that once this was over she could resume her old position in the company and go back to being friendly little Rosa?

Otillio told her to go home. However, he noticed while he was there, that there was a beat up car parked about twenty yards from the entrance to the store. It was a bit far, considering there were several spots much closer where they could have parked but didn't. During the course of the 30 minutes that they were talking, Otillio saw the passenger, a man, get out of the car and go into the store twice—only to come out empty-handed both times. Finally, the older woman, the driver of the car, got out and did the same. When they got back home, Otillio asked his cousins if they had observed the car and the odd behavior of its occupants. They had indeed, and in fact, they had the license number of the vehicle.

As Otillio's family discussed the situation, no one had any doubt that Rosa was involved up to her ankles—head first! Otillio did his best to be impartial. He never liked Rosa, never trusted her and so far as it seemed his judgment of her had been right on the money—in more ways than one!

CHAPTER SIX
Day Five

I think what saved my sanity throughout this entire ordeal was that I never stopped planning. I constantly planned my escape. It was really quite elaborate, especially for a man who had, by this time, been confined to a chair for five days. What was I thinking? Like my wobbly legs and weakened body was suddenly going to turn into super ninja, and I would bound out of the house high kicking the faces and chests of my captors. Remembering my thoughts now, leads me to believe I suffered far more hallucinations than I thought at the time. But, the planning continued. I planned what I would do to these scumbags when I escaped. It was no sketchy plan, either. I had plenty of time to plan in detail—vivid detail. In my mind I beat them all, I tortured them, half starved them and mapped out in great detail what I was doing to their families! There was nothing beyond my capabilities. When the anger wore me out, I thought of my family and planned how I would be a better husband and father to them. As much as I tried to fight the depression, often during that day, I planned my own death. I wondered if it could possibly hurt any more than what I had already been through.

Every time I was tempted to settle into thoughts of my own death, the need to survive would break through, and I would find just a glimmer of hope buried deep down to see me through just a few more hours. Surely, they would come in just a few more hours. How much could one man endure?

"Okay, Ken, enough of the vague planning," I repeated in my mind. "You've got to come up with something concrete." I had to quit waiting for somebody to come save me. "Look, you got yourself into this mess—now it's up to you to get yourself out of it!" This was more of the tough stuff I said to myself. I ordered my body to respond to my mental demands. I never had been accustomed to taking no for an answer, and it was difficult for me to accept the fact that my body just wasn't going to fully comply!

More and more, I requested to use the bathroom. It wasn't so much for the use of the facilities; although a steamy shower, white fluffy towels, the clean smell of soap and fresh clothing wasn't a bad idea. However, my need to get to the bathroom was really to test my limbs, to see my surroundings, to gauge my strength and the possibilities of making a getaway.

I was beginning to feel like a prisoner of war, and in a way maybe I was. These people were in a war, planning their escape as desperately as I was. Theirs was a need to escape the hopelessness of poverty, the mindless labor for meager wages that imprisoned them and their families. I can rationalize those things now that I lay here in this hospital bed; but at the time, all the compassion had been beaten from me. What was left was resentment and hatred, fear and disgust! After all, many Mexican people were in the same boat as these *desperadoes*—even worse, and they hadn't resorted to kidnapping, torture and what could eventually end up being murder.

When my mind tired of thinking about my game plan, I would merely sit and listen. For hours on end, I'd listen for even the slightest of movements. Bugs buzzing around my secretions. They provided a form of torture equally as overpowering as my captors. They too were going for blood. What if I caught malaria, or some such dreaded disease? What if my captors couldn't get the money and they just left me in this chair to die of exposure to thousands of ants, mosquitoes and flies? What if the last my family saw of me were pictures sent by the police of a half-eaten, bug-infested, unrecognizable body that used to be me?

"God, don't think of those things, Ken," I admonished myself. "Just listen for life—listen for clues that will help you to identify your assailants when the time comes for them to face the music! Listen for clues to where you are; who is in the room with you; when to move just one tiny little finger without drawing the displeasure of the guard." So, I listened—for hours I listened, thinking that perhaps my bodyguard was either asleep or in another room. When I thought the way was clear, ever so softly, I would wiggle.

"Boom—ssshhh—boom!" In a flash he was up in my face, with his threatening, humid breath blanketing me. I moved—he yelled. I moved my head to satisfy an itch—he slammed my head back against the chair with the side of the gun. I whispered a plea for release—he fired the gun into the ceiling. We played variations of the same game countless times, but I never won. Each morning, my friend the rooster would awaken me to the horrors of the day and the hope that this day someone would save me from this living hell.

As time went on, my captors became quite confident that they would not be discovered. I was sure, during the hottest hours of the day, that they would leave the doors open in hopes of encouraging a crosswind. What if I shouted, begging one of the children outside or the workers coming home from a hard day's labor—what if I shouted out, begging them for my life? I figured it wouldn't do me much good since they probably wouldn't be able to understand me, anyway. Besides, it might only serve to get that filthy rag shoved back into my mouth, and then the gagging and nausea would start. I feared once that started, there'd be no stopping me then.

The morning had started with the familiar signal. It was nothing complicated; I'm not sure any of them were smart enough to remember a complex signal. Just a tap at the rear window followed by the sound of the door that allowed the visitor entrance. That morning, as usual, I heard the signal; but unlike many of the previous mornings, there were additional voices, more activity. Something was in the air—a feeling of anticipation that today would be different. I waited, trying to act as if I were unaware of any of the increased excitement or eager behavior.

Soon, I felt the presence of several people in the room. Don't ask me how I knew there were more than one; perhaps by their added body heat felt on the rawness of my blistered and bitten skin. Perhaps, like a blind man, I was beginning to rely more and more on my instincts, my hearing and what that inner voice told me to be true. I cut my pupils around from corner to corner under the tight blindfold, but my efforts were fruitless. I saw nothing—not even a shadow cross my path or a single beam of light. The blindfold was kept so tight that it cut into my face, allowing not even the penetration of my own sticky blood to more than cake over its surface. At times, I imagined its weight significantly increased and heard the feasting efforts of the latest bug banquet held in my honor, right across the blindfold. Nasty! This was a nasty business with no relief in sight!

Suddenly, before I could fully understand what was happening, I heard them fumbling with something that sounded like a video game. Then, their voices were raised in anger as one yelled at the other and snatched away the game. Try as I might, I just couldn't figure out what they were doing. "Playing with a game? How could they afford games? Was this game worth all the torture they had put me through?" I wondered, almost hysterical, at the thought that the life was being sucked out of me for some stupid video game!

"*Señor*, do this!" They were taking my blindfold off. Here was the moment I had waited for. I felt something being laid across my thighs. "You call—call Otillio!" the man ordered.

All this time I had thought of little else but having this offensive blindfold removed and being able to identify my captors, and now I couldn't even open up my burning, dry eyes to the fire of the sunlight. The game began again—they beat me and ordered me to open my eyes, I tried to do the impossible. God, all this light—this blinding light was worse than being blindfolded. My eyes were matted tightly together, and one of my tormentors reached down to pry them open.

There was a pop sound, like the cap to a ketchup-caked container being pried open. First one eye then the other.

The tears were running down my cheeks, and the shadows surrounding me were now pointing this game at me, yelling, "Call—call now!"

I could barely make out the silhouette forms hovering over me, but the game they shoved in my untied hand was one I recognized. It was my precious link to life—my cell phone. With patience and persistence, I coaxed my eyes to focus on that cell phone, hoping there was a voice from home at the other end. I willed my stiffened fingers to stretch out and receive its promise. They slapped it in my hand, but I couldn't make my fingers obey—they simply curled back into the position they'd been in for the past gazillion years, which was that of being partially curved around hardened pencils under them as they were strapped to the wooden chair. It was an instinctive return to what they knew.

Next, they laid my address/day planner across my legs. Its smooth leather was cool to the touch, and I found its presence somewhat comforting. It was a reminder that I was not a caged animal buried in its own waste. I was a successful businessman; I had many friends and business associates as evidenced by the many names staring up at me from my telephone directory inside the day planner. But, that life seemed far away, one that perhaps I would never go back to.

As the tears cleared, and my eyes centered on the printed page, I saw Otillio's office number. They had been attempting to call him, but had no luck getting the phone to work. As luck would have it, this was my U.S. cell phone. It

Terror In Mexico:
The Kidnapping of Ken Krusensterna

worked about as good in Mexico as tits on a bull. I noticed, though, that the battery was still good; it had been turned off all this time. I felt as though I was losing my edge—and hysteria began to set in as I contemplated the situation. Here were these kidnappers who were too stupid to figure out a cell phone. They were all dressed in black, and I thought to myself that we had something in common after all—the need to ninja out!

I was glad to finally be untied, to see the room and my captors, yet fearing they would think I was trying to trick them, I fiddled with the phone for a while as if I were surprised that it wouldn't work. "No signal," I said to them.

"Otillio!" one of the meanest of the group shouted. Then he pointed the gun in the air and fired off a shot or two for emphasis. I can tell you that would have done it for me a few days ago, but I was used to their antics by this time, and I gave up the notion of explaining to them why the phone wouldn't work. With their limited knowledge of English, by the time I could explain the cell phone to them, there'd be no more need for the damn thing.

"I cannot call him. There is no signal." I tried to speak slowly, talk softly so as not to anger the mean one. It didn't matter much, though. I still got a slam on the head.

"*Señor*! Call Otillio, now!"

I wanted to yell out, "God damnit, you bastard, call him yourself if you're so smart!" No matter how I tried, I couldn't get these idiots to understand that sometimes you are in an area so remote, the cellular signal just won't reach. The game was over for now. They finally gave up and took the phone away. I had left it on, however, in hopes of what I don't know. Could they track a cell phone signal? It was a desperate attempt to convince myself that there was still hope.

The nerves in my arm were beginning to come alive with an incredible burning sensation and points of pain jabbing me in every single nerve. After tying me back up and replacing the blindfold, the men left the room. I had nothing to concentrate on now but the overwhelming pain shooting up my arm into my neck. I ground my teeth to keep them from chattering as the symptoms of shock set back in. Flames of pain licked at the muscles of my arm until I fell into blessed unconsciousness.

* * *

As exhausted and tortured as I was, my family was going through a torment of their own. Beth awaited her flight to our family home in Dallas on Sunday and tried as hard as she could to function in her normal, everyday routine of caring for the horses on her small holding in Phoenix. Unfortunately for Beth, she had inherited my impatience—my need to go full-steam-ahead plowing through the red tape and challenges of what others thought was impossible in order to get the job done.

This is what frustrated Beth so much; she knew it was no time to act like her dad—the job wasn't to get done by the hot-headedness she felt and the temper tantrums lying just below her fixed expression and controlled behavior. Her work suffered the Friday she went to work before leaving on Sunday. She could concentrate on nothing except what she wanted to do to the fuckers who had taken her dad. She spent the entire day dropping things and forgetting instructions given to her. Just like me, Beth was a prisoner of her fears and over-worked imagination.

That Friday evening, she stopped by the Circle K to buy a beer. That seemed to be the ticket—drink herself into oblivion until she flew to Dallas on Sunday. Just about the time she thought this, she stepped from the curb and fell flat on her ass. Hell, she wasn't even drunk yet! Nothing was working for her, and drinking wasn't going to do anything but deepen her sorrow at the thought that she might lose her dad.

By Saturday morning, the sorrow had turned to downright angry belligerence. She just couldn't sit by and do nothing. Beth's fiancee, Jerry, understood her well, so he did the only thing he knew would let her escape her tormented thoughts. He saddled up her favorite steed and encouraged her to ride off into the brisk November desert air. When she almost rode that horse to the ground, Beth returned to saddle another—and another—and another. She just kept on riding all day and far into the evening. She didn't eat and didn't even get out of the saddle except to exchange one mount for another. No food, no water, just speed and endurance to distract her from her fears and build hatred for those dirty slime buckets that had her dad.

Meanwhile, Deanne and Corinne had been holding down the fort at home. Not having recovered from her severe illness, Corinne was kept in a daze. Everybody thought it best to curb her worry and numb her mental anguish with medication, so the doctors recommended she remain in bed as much as possible. As strong as she normally was, there was only so much one small, petite woman could handle—no matter how tough she would have liked to think she was. As thorough and organized as she could be, her thoughts were chaotic, confused, dazed. This was one of the most difficult times for Corinne since it is her nature to fix things, make everything perfect and make her family happy. That was number one to Corinne, but now she was helpless to do anything but fall into a drug-induced fitful slumber.

The kids exchanged stories to make the time pass. Keeping the memory of their father alive, they remembered when we had moved to Wisconsin to open the hotel, and Corinne had taken it upon herself to make everything perfect by fixing things for the guests. It was understood when it came to the hotel that I made things happen; Corinne made things special! They remembered one time in particular when a couple who were regulars at another hotel stopped by to look at ours. They hadn't even known we were there until others mentioned us to them. They told Corinne that they always came up to Wisconsin for their anniversary. Corinne just listened, encouraging them to share the joys of their relationship. When they left, she high-tailed it into town and got some small bottles of Asti Spumante with other little niceties in celebration of their special day. She knew they'd come back, and they did. When they stepped inside the door, Corinne warmly welcomed them, saying, "I've got your room all ready for you!"

"How did you know we'd come back?" they asked.

"I just know people. I hoped you'd come stay with us and share this lovely occasion, and I wanted to make everything just right for you." Because of Corinne, our little hotel flourished, and we prospered. The kids knew that our success was owed more to Corinne's personal touches than to my business dealings.

As the hours drug on, the kids' reminiscing was brought to a halt when FBI agents crowded the living room and wandered through the house to use the bathroom and make themselves at home. Shawn, the case agent, had gotten all the details from the kids and briefed them on what to do when the phone rang. Deanne and Keith, when he was there, had scripts to work from. Each performed their parts brilliantly, and I was never so proud of them as when I laid recovering in the hospital hearing the stories of their courage and stamina.

I'm sure it had to be awkward for them to have total strangers in our home for the duration, but there was little else that could be done. Corinne worried that our neighbors might get suspicious that something was going on and report some kind of drug activity or something. Or, what if one of the captors was watching the house and saw a police car pull up or witnessed all the plain-clothed professionals swarming the grounds? It was quite unusual to see all this commotion around our home. We are simple folks who just kind of keep to ourselves, rarely partying. One thing for sure, we didn't often have tall, well-built, dark-suited men regularly visiting our home in shifts!

They were all wishing that I had given everyone a more detailed itinerary. They weren't the only ones! If I had, they might have been able to narrow the search to within a few-mile radius at least. Corinne was so trusting and so busy, that she never questioned much. She had her end to carry, and I had mine. As I heard their stories unfold one-by-one, I felt I had let them all down.

They, surely, couldn't say the same for themselves. Keith had taken a crash course in becoming an FBI agent himself. The burden was his to be the liaison for the family. I can just picture him—his adult frame surrounding his baby face. He would sit and listen carefully to everything the FBI said, making few, if any, comments. Then he would ponder; put it all together, and say, "Okay, I got it." That was Keith. I'm sure Keith was not fully aware of the importance of his position in all this, but one screw up by him and my life could have been gone forever. Even though he was so young in chronological age, Keith was a man in his thoughts and actions during this entire affair. He was up for the challenge.

* * *

In Mexico, there were others to consider besides myself and my abductors—there was Otillio and his family. Not knowing whether this kidnapping had been a personal vendetta or strictly business, Otillio dealt with his own fears. He and his family had been hiding out, moving from one place to another just in case they were being followed. He feared for his safety, but his real concern was for his wife and children. He was limited as to how deep he could go underground, because the only contact number that Rosa had was Otillio's cell phone. That Saturday morning, Rosa decided to use it!

Terror In Mexico:
The Kidnapping of Ken Krusensterna

"Please Otillio. You must meet me!"

"Where are you, Rosa?" he asked.

"I am in my car."

Well that gave him a big clue as to her whereabouts! "I thought I told you to stay put!" Otillio said, aggravated that she had put him in this position. From day one, Otillio had never trusted Rosa, and now she had involved him and endangered his family.

"I need to speak with you, Otillio." This was just great. He knew that he needed to do anything he could to help save me, but at the same time, he didn't want to risk messing up the investigation or putting his own safety in jeopardy. "No, I'm sorry, Rosa. I cannot meet with you."

"Why—God, Otillio—you must!"

"I refuse. I don't know who these people are, and you cannot guarantee my safety or that of my *familia*!"

"What if I meet you at the office?" she offered. Otillio thought about it. He didn't really see a problem; our office was occupied twenty-four/seven! He was confident it would be safer there than anywhere else since there were plenty of people around—even on a Saturday.

"Okay, we can meet there," he agreed. Still not trusting her, Otillio asked the same cousins to follow him and search for signs of that same car, the one they had seen lurking around Rosa at the previous meeting. His cousins were like Otillio's insurance policy—there to make sure he remained a free man—ready to do whatever it took. The drive to the office took him about twenty minutes, and he caught himself watching his back every moment. Even the enclosure of the car couldn't make him feel entirely protected.

Rosa was waiting, and not so patiently, when Otillio arrived at the office. She reached out to him as if to give him a sympathetic hug, but he backed off from her. Not only did he not want her to touch him, but he wanted no possibility that she would plant something on him that would lead his enemies straight back to his family. His aversion to Rosa was so complete that she couldn't help but notice. But, there was no comment about it before they got down to the business of why she had requested this meeting.

Everything happened as if in slow motion, but Otillio's mind was working overtime. He wanted to remember every detail for the family and the FBI. As he carefully examined her appearance, he couldn't help but recognize how much calmer and well put together she looked. Her hair had been freshly washed and carefully styled. Her eyes looked rested and clear of the redness that had been there upon their first meeting. This was certainly not the look of a woman whose beloved mother was being held by ruthless kidnappers. This was the look of a businesswoman ready to do some tough negotiations.

"Thank you for coming, Otillio."

"What is it you need?" he questioned, impatient with the small talk. He wanted her to get to the point and let him get the hell out of there.

"I . . . um . . . got a call from Keith."

"Yes, so . . ."

"He has agreed to meet me, but I am scared to go there."

"Why, Rosa—you have no reason to be afraid of Keith."

Terror In Mexico:
The Kidnapping of Ken Krusensterna

"He wants me to go to the U.S. side to meet him."

"But, you have done that so many times before. What makes this so difficult for you?"

"I . . . I've never had to come face-to-face with a family member of Ken's before."

"Well, if the two of you are just trying to get Ken back, then you're on the same side. Keith won't hurt you."

"I am also afraid that I may be taken," she finally revealed.

"Why would you think that, Rosa? Aren't you an innocent victim as well?" Otillio was playing with her while observing her discomfort and what she was going to pull next.

"Of course, but what if the *policía* think I am involved? I will be put in prison, no?"

"Why would they think that?"

"I . . . well, I do not know. Who knows what people think? I just don't know about the American legal system."

"We both know it is more just than ours! You are safe there if you have done nothing wrong!" he said, wanting to leave her with that additional fear in hopes that she might confess her involvement.

"Do you know if the *policía* have been called by Ken's *familia*?" she asked.

"I have separated myself from all this, Rosa, so I really cannot say. But, why would you think they had?" Otillio asked, trying to discover exactly what she knew.

"Yesterday, when I went to the store, someone followed me the whole time. I am sure of it!"

"Maybe you are just being paranoid, or maybe it's the kidnappers wanting to make sure you don't call the police," he

80

answered. Inside his anger was building. He was more sure than ever of her involvement. Then he began asking himself, "What if someone had notified the authorities? What if the Mexican *officianados* had been called in? What if they were actually involved themselves?

"I know what you are thinking, Otillio, but I am not involved with his. I am just afraid that people will not believe me. I am afraid if I go onto American soil, I will not be safe from captivity by their police!"

"Well, I guess if you really want to see your mother free again, as well as Ken, you'll have to do what is required of you. Keith is the only one who can get you the money."

"I am like a pawn in their game. I feel used! I have no choice but to put my own life in danger." With that, they parted ways. As Otillio drove home, he pondered all of the information he had been privy to and was sure that Rosa had secrets to protect. Her calm demeanor didn't ring true to the highly emotional state he knew she would be in if it were true that her mother were being held by *desperadoes*. Rosa was a smart girl—but a lousy kidnapper!

CHAPTER SEVEN
The Interrogation

"How much longer would my body hold out? Better yet, how much longer could my mind take this kind of punishment?" It had been several days now, and my thoughts were not as clear as they had been just the day before. "Jesus," I prayed, "what could be the problem? They want money—I have money! Just give them the shit and get me out of here!" I reasoned, confused as to why nobody was here for me when I so desperately needed them.

Then the questions started again. Did they even know I was there? Had they called the police? Were they trying to get the money and arrange an exchange? Even now, my sense of humor would creep in and surprise my depression— Were they all on a Caribbean Cruise, enjoying their inheritance? But, humor was soon replaced with the dark thoughts, and I wondered if it would be too late when the ransom demands could be met. Nothing to do now but wait— wait—wait—endless waiting!

"What to do to take my mind of this waiting?" I questioned, deciding that a busy mind was much more preferable to one that was left to its own devices. During the evening, the captors had come, I think, to tighten my straps and secure my neck hold, but I felt nothing. Suddenly, I was jolted into a state of sheer panic. As I tested my toes on up to my neck, I realized that I could no longer feel my right arm. "My arm is gone—Jesus, they've cut off my arm! Those sons of bitches have cut off my arm and sent it to my family!" I had heard similar stories of kidnappers who had cut off the ears of their young victims and mailed them home as proof. I had read about another bandit who had mailed home the little finger of his victim, a friendly little reminder to consider this the first shipment if the money wasn't received within three days.

"What was with these kidnappers, anyway? Did they think we were all rich, miracle workers who were able to scrounge up hundreds of thousands of dollars in a day or two? Obviously so, by the sound of things around me; they were angry at the fact that things were not going as planned!"

Once again, my wandering mind focused on my right limb—the one that I was convinced had been cut off. I could feel the stickiness of my blood dripping on my foot, and I wondered how they would keep me from bleeding to death. In actuality, they hadn't cut off anything. I couldn't feel that arm any longer; I couldn't wriggle my fingers or confirm its presence in anyway because its pain had been replaced by sheer and complete numbness. The stickiness that I was feeling was sweat, which at this point with my suffering severe dehydration was almost as precious as blood.

I still had a bit of feeling in my other arm, so I just knew that my right one had been cut off. "Face it, Ken, if you survive this, you'll be a cripple all your life." I wanted to lash out. How would I function with just one arm? I wouldn't be able to pilot my plane, play golf, swim, ride horses, even drive a truck. Now I was getting angry. I wanted to kill them for permanently altering my life like that. Even if I couldn't get them all, I could down one or two of them before they could finish me off!

About the time all those kind thoughts were circling in my mind, in they came like a pack of wild wolves, closer and closer, smelling their prey—coming in for the kill. I had thought of my own little pet names for them. Let's see—there was the sexpot cooker, diarrhea mouth and Mr. Military. It sounded like they were all present and counted for. The televisions, which blared their meaningless chatter throughout the house, were on loud as ever, only now I could hear that familiar voice of Pat Summerall again. "Hi Pat," I spoke to myself. He'd never know what good friends we had become. I had listened to him for years, so I knew now that it was Sunday and the stations were tuned in to American football.

It's amazing how football can soothe the savage beast; but I have to confess, I never thought it would see me through a kidnapping—especially my own. Ah, all the comforts of home. Here I was in my chair with my little football treats of a half-filled Dixie cup of water and a few bites of a banana. What more could a fellow ask for? Of course, there was nobody to take bets over the score with me, and the Mexican translator was yacking away, rudely interrupting all Pat's lively telecast, but it was great to hear my own language.

Remembering our usual Sunday afternoon activity of coaching the football game from my living room chair was comforting—making me feel closer to my family and the country I loved. If I ever got out of this, I'd appreciate them both much more than ever before. Regardless of the reasons, I clung to Pat's anticipation of the game and the roar of the crowds. I rallied a bit, knowing that there were still some people enjoying the normalcy of a regular Sunday afternoon. Even these animals could set aside their troubles for the battle on the football field.

The game took me away for a few hours, and afterwards I let my mind wander. What would I do if I ever got out of here? Well, perhaps I could do all those things I loved with a prosthetic arm. After all, there were plenty of people who managed quite well missing a limb. I wanted to scratch my left arm so badly, but I didn't have an arm to do that with anymore. I hoped they would stop there—amputating only my arm. The dripping had stopped, so I hoped I wouldn't bleed to death.

Maybe it would have been a blessing had my entire body gone numb, then I wouldn't have felt the paint of the chair continuing to eat into my flesh. I wouldn't have felt my cramped muscles knot and twist in agony. I wouldn't have needed to shrug my shoulder to try to itch my bearded face and risk getting another beating. Now, I didn't pray for escape—I prayed for numbness, for oblivion, for unconsciousness or sleep.

I dozed off again and my thoughts were back on my family. What were they doing now? Surely they had to know of the demons' demands. Would they know what to do?

* * *

Sunday had finally come, and Beth was ready to fly to Dallas to be with the rest of the family. She'd made arrangements with her friend to come and do the mid-day feedings for the horses. Jerry would do them in the mornings and evenings when he got home from work. Knowing that it could be a while before her return, she set up all the bills and paid them methodically. Beth had no idea how long she would be gone, but she knew her father wouldn't want her to let her business fall apart while she was in Dallas. They both had that need to be a success no matter what their endeavor, and Beth was proud to have followed in her father's footsteps.

Beth's flight seemed like it lasted a lifetime but was no longer than the usual flight from Phoenix to Dallas. Larry met her at the airport; they hugged each other and exchanged the comfort from their shared tears and soothing voices. As she looked around the airport, Beth realized others were having tearful reunions as well, but probably none were as dramatic as what they were all experiencing.

How could life go on so normally? How could people be flying to make out-of-town business meetings or vacation with their friends and family? Beth looked at the signs of happiness around her and found herself unreasonably resenting them all. How could they? How could they go through their days as if this was not happening to her family and her father? Life just wasn't fair anymore—not like when she had been a kid who was protected in the innocence that she and her family would always be safe and secure.

All the way home, Beth pummeled Larry with one question after another. "What in the hell is going on, anyway?" she'd ask.

"They've made demands for a ransom," Larry informed her, fearing her next logical question.

"How much do the ass holes want?"

"They've demanded $350,000 and have even gone so far as to request $100,000 of it in *pesos*."

"My God, these bastards are bold! Well, did we get it yet?"

"No, we're going to try and stall them." Now Larry really expected the shit to hit the fan, and it did!

"What do you mean, stall them? We're talking about my dad's life here. Stall them? Give the fuckers what they want, then when they come to pick it up blow them away! No, don't blow them away; kill them slow—torture them for the same number of days they have my father. Stall them? Jesus Christ!"

"Beth, you haven't been here. You don't know everything that's gone on."

"I know enough to know that we should have had him back by now. The stall is off—as of this minute. Stall them— you're going to have to stall me from going over there and finding him myself!"

"Look, the agents feel . . ."

"What agents?"

"The FBI agents. They're in on this now."

"Oh great. That means some asshole is going to be hanging around most of the time when our family's dealing with this crisis . . . trying to tell us what to do?"

"Um . . . not just some of the time. They're in your parents' home around the clock. They're doing what they have to do, Beth." Larry was another calming force in this whole situation. He had been a friend of our family for so long, he seemed like an uncle to my kids. He had moved with me from company to company, and I was always glad to have him contributing to my next business venture.

"Larry, please explain what you mean by stalling, then!" she pushed.

"It's Sunday. Banks don't open until Monday. They have to be reasonable and give us some time to come up with that amount of money."

"Oh, and you're just sure these are reasonable, rational human beings, right? Poor people who have nothing and need food and clothing for their dozen kids? Larry, my family is going to have to wake up and smell the roses, or the shit fertilizing the roses."

"Calm down now, Beth. It's not going to do your mom or anyone a bit of good for you to be this upset at the house. Your mom needs her kids to be level-headed right now. You can do that; I know you can!"

"It's . . . hard . . . that's all, Larry. He's my dad . . ." and her voice broke with her building emotional state. Beth would have died for me, and I know it. However, she jokingly told me later that her negative attitude toward all the FBI agents changed drastically, when they got to the house, and she saw that one of them looked like Brad Pitt. They later teased me that Beth finally came to a new understanding of "stalling" after she asked Mr. Pitt to explain things to her in great detail—way into the evening—and give her comfort in her hours and hours of need! In reality, Beth tried to contain her highly emotional heart, but every once in a while she could do nothing but rant and cry, rant and cry.

It was awkward between the girls for a while. Beth wanted answers right away, and Deanne had been dealing with everything for too long. Now that I look back on things, she may have been a bit resentful of that. She got tired of answering Beth's questions even though Beth had a right to know what had happened during her absence. Beth, in turn, felt frustrated and left out at Deanne's expressions of exasperation at having to answer questions that seemed to lead in circles and had little to do with the possibilities of getting their father out of Mexico alive.

The two girls were six years apart in age and complete opposites in personality. It caused some friction that would flare up from time to time, but generally all the kids worked together to make this bearable. Corinne sat numbly by and waited for the word that I had been found and was on my way home. She never showed she was scared and was rock solid. She said later that she always felt in her heart everything would work out, and I would make it back to them.

As the women talked, Keith planned. He worked feverishly with the FBI for about three days. He and Maria, one of the FBI agents who did a lot of the translating work, were soon on their way back down to McAllen. Keith had been going over scripts and was quizzed and drilled at every turn about what to say and how to deal with psychotic kidnappers. But, they all knew there was no sane way to deal with the crazy mentality of these people. All this could be for nothing—all their efforts could still go bad!

The FBI had set up a satellite office in a RV in McAllen. From this station, much of the investigations took place and it was the central calling post. The electronic equipment was set up there in an attempt to trace calls coming to various cell phones. Messages moved in and out of the RV, but the family despaired that nothing short of miracle was going to get their dad back home again.

If it was miracles they needed, it would be miracles they created. Maria and Keith arrived at headquarters in McAllen and placed a call to Rosa. Since Maria was Hispanic, she was better able to communicate. Rosa was surprised that she could not play the simple-minded foreigner anymore by pretending ignorance of the language. Maria introduced herself as a family friend trying to get more details for them, so they could be assured that their father was alive and would be returned as soon as the money was paid. Rosa fell for the story and began to spill her guts, not realizing her many indiscretions and inconsistencies as she spoke casually in her native tongue:

"So, tell me again, the story," Maria asked.

"I was just coming home . . ." And, there she went with the same tired song and dance she had been giving everyone. She seemed to just chatter along, like it was everyday conversation. However, Maria knew the story down to the minutest of details as Rosa had told it before; we had it on tape. She was an incredibly sharp detective, and Keith's hope to find his father alive increased with every encounter he had with Maria at the helm. She was a sharp, yet sensitive, agent who asked just the right questions with just the right emphasis—making them seem casual and unplanned. Rosa couldn't hold her a candle to go by.

"Tell me how they released you." Maria encouraged her to speak, acting as if she felt sorry for her and her mother.

"They just dropped me off in town."

"When was that, Rosa? Do you remember about what time of day it was?" Maria knew Rosa had said it was after dark the first time.

"It was in the middle of the day. They just dropped me in town."

"So, I can't remember, how did you say you got home?"

"I just took a car. I didn't think anyone would mind, considering what I had gone through, you know. But, they must have come and gotten it later. I didn't know much by then, you know."

"Oh, so you didn't recognize the car you took? It didn't belong to any one you know?"

"No, it was a stranger's." Another change in the story! By the time they were done, Maria was completely convinced that Rosa was no innocent, and everybody agreed. She may have been coerced into doing this, although that, too, was doubtful, but she was a part of it and had the ability to make it end. Then, Maria went in for the kill. Let's just see how desperate these people are for the money. She had set up the meeting that Rosa was dreading. She convinced Rosa to come to the U.S. to meet with Keith and her, and together they would talk about the demands of the kidnappers.

After the call, Rosa called Otillio and was visibly upset by the fact that she might be exposed. Otillio was in a very difficult position, though. He knew that if anything happened to me, he might be blamed. He also considered himself to be a suspect, although no one in my family ever seriously thought that to be a possibility. He was constantly watching his back. He was concerned about the criminals, the authorities and what my family might do next that could endanger my life even further. For his own safety, he asked another friend to drive him over to the United States side of the border. They both, Otillio and his friend, had the proper paperwork to enable them to come and go relatively easily, and they crossed the bridges without a hitch.

The meetings were set, and the Holiday Inn acted as host to the gathering. FBI had "staged" a room by preparing it for surveillance. Everything that was said in that room would be monitored and taped.

Otillio and his friend arrived about 8:30 in the morning. When they got to the room, Otillio noticed a woman with Keith, and he suspected this was more than just a meeting to discover how the exchange was to be made. However, he was innocent of any wrongdoing, and he hoped Keith would recognize that fact. All he wanted was for Ken to come home safe and sound and for business to get on as usual. He had no idea that after something like this, business never goes on as usual—nor should it. After having experienced such dangers, it stands to reason people are unable to just pick up where they left off, carry on as usual and pretend it never happened.

Keith approached Otillio and his friend and asked the friend to wait outside while they talked. In some respects, Otillio took exception to this since Keith's friend was allowed to stay. But, it wasn't his dad who had been kidnapped and was facing death. He figured it was Keith's right to call the shots.

For the next couple of hours, Maria questioned Otillio about everything that had transpired up to this point. I'm sure he was sick of repeating it, just like everyone else, but he knew it was his duty to help me get home.

Chapter Seven:
The Interrogation

"How did Ken get hooked up with this Rosa girl and her mother?" Maria questioned.

"He met the little girl through his Mexican attorney, Ricardo," answered Otillio. He always referred to Rosa as "little girl," which Corinne said made her sound like some 12-year-old who would be incapable of planning the kidnapping.

"So, he didn't know her before they became business associates, correct?"

"No, he needed someone to set up the company, and she came highly recommended."

"Did she spend much time in the office?"

"Well, she did a lot of the translating for Ken. She would accompany him on several business dinners and meetings with Mexican businessmen and made a very professional appearance."

"Did you like her, Otillio?" The question struck him as odd, but he had to answer honestly.

"No. I didn't like her and I didn't trust her."

"Why?"

"It's just one of those feelings you can get when you know something or someone is not right. I had it in the pit of my stomach."

"Did you ever warn Ken about Rosa?"

"I think so. I mean, Ken is pretty stubborn. They had a good business set up; he didn't want to rock the boat."

"Do you know how she was paid?"

"Too much, if you ask me! She got a luxury apartment; one that cost the equivalent of about $2,500 per month in American money. She got a new minivan, and I think Ken's company even paid for her father's hospital bills when he suffered a heart attack. On top of that, they gave her some spending money to supplement her "clothing business."

By the time they were done talking, Maria had ruled Otillio out as a suspect, and she was even more convinced that Rosa was the culprit. Otillio, too, was certain that Maria was more than just a friend! He suspected her to be a law enforcement officer or some sort of government agent. He was relieved to see that they had taken his advice to get the government involved. Again I go back to the feeling that everybody was playing a game, and I was the prize! The next step was to wait for Rosa to show her face—if she dared. It would be a test to see which emotion was the strongest—greed or fear! Now it was Rosa's turn to be interrogated, only her interrogators would be clever enough to catch her at her own game before she'd know what hit her.

CHAPTER EIGHT
Discovery

Maria wasn't too far into the questioning process with Rosa when she realized she was in it deeper than cow shit in a slaughterhouse. We all had to give her credit, though, Rosa sure could act. Little did she know that she never had to resort to kidnapping; she could have made a much better living as a Hollywood actress.

When Rosa entered the hotel room that had been specially prepared for her performance, she immediately became suspicious at Maria's presence. "Who is this?" she asked Keith, tilting her head in Maria's direction.

"Her name is Maria, and she's a family friend who understands Spanish. I've told her about my father, and she offered to help."

"I don't understand why she is here; how can she help?" Rosa questioned further with the telltale fear rising in her voice.

"She's here because I don't speak a lick of Spanish, and I really didn't know how good your English is." That seemed to placate her for a while. She was crying, and without the experienced eye of a trained officer, it might have been difficult to tell they were token tears. Emotion

Terror In Mexico:
The Kidnapping of Ken Krusensterna

free-flowed throughout the room as the tapes rolled, recording every word of her fake caring and inaccurate sequence of events. A few more mistakes—a few more holes, but by this time the questions were more to put her at a disadvantage where she might unintentionally relay some valuable information. It was no secret; Rosa was involved up to her eyeballs, but she kept rambling and was totally unaware of their disbelief. "I just want my Mama and Ken to get out of this alive. They are very bad men!" she sobbed.

"I'm sure you do," thought Keith. "Or it would be murder instead of kidnapping, you little bitch!" He wasn't fooled. Keith told me later that at first she had a few convincing moments, especially back at the office on Friday when she looked as though she had really been crying. The more she talked, however, the more certain he became of her guilt! Keith is a smart boy! He doesn't always say a whole lot, but he knows how to keep his mouth shut and listen.

Meanwhile, Maria was closely observing Rosa. What she did was almost as informative as what she said. She could keep up the soft, innocent routine for a while, but then a certain hardness would creep in; her voice would harden and her demeanor would stiffen. Sure she was afraid, and rightfully so! She definitely appeared nervous, but was it out of fear for her mother or fear for her own freedom? Maria guessed it was the later. "Where are they keeping Ken?" Maria asked.

"Oh, I do not know that! I was blindfolded the whole time—you remember."

"Well, something confuses me here, Rosa. How did you know he was in bad shape, if you were blindfolded the whole time?"

"Um . . . well . . . I could just tell by his voice that he was weak. Ken is a very strong man. He never want to show weakness, you know?"

"I was also wondering," Maria continued, as if she'd just thought of something else, "how you managed to get him all those drinks of water? You know, if you were tied and blindfolded and all!"

"Well . . . I was untied by that point, and I just asked them in my native tongue to get us drinks of water, which I shared with Ken." She was quick, but her responses didn't really make sense.

As they spoke, Maria translated so Keith could understand. Unable to contain himself any further, Keith stepped in. Eager to see her reaction, he looked into her eyes as he spoke the next question. "I need for you to tell them that I don't have the money!"

"What do you mean, you don't have the money?" Rosa starred at Keith a bit too long and too confidently, almost angrily, before she caught herself and returned to acting the victim.

"I mean . . . they demanded money on a Friday afternoon. Our banks are closed here until Monday, Rosa."
"Oh," she responded, almost relieved. "Well, when should I tell them that you will have it?"

"I'm going to see what I can do tomorrow, but they've got to give me some time. I don't have my dad's signature, and he's the one who could always get cash." The next thing

Terror In Mexico:
The Kidnapping of Ken Krusensterna

they did was very clever. The kidnappers had been able to use the cell phone that Rosa had on her to make the previous calls. We were aware that they couldn't use my U.S. phone, and the FBI needed a phone they could trace. Don't ask me how, but somehow Maria talked Rosa into giving her the cell phone. From that point on, the kidnappers would have to make their demands from a payphone to my home phone in Dallas, and the FBI could then trace the calls.

"I'm a little concerned about something," Rosa said, in her "little girl" voice.

"What's that?" Maria answered.

"I am afraid that the officials know something."

"Why do you say that?" Keith asked, fearing that she might have some real information that could hurt his dad.

"Because someone has followed me on more than one occasion."

"How do you know it's not the kidnappers?" asked Maria.

"I can just tell; it was not the kidnappers."

At the end of the meeting, it was decided that Rosa would go back and wait at home for the kidnappers to call her. Then she would have them call Keith the next day. That done, Rosa said her good-byes to Maria and Keith and left the Holiday Inn for home.

Then Maria and Keith and those listening to the tapes got down to some serious discussion. They analyzed just who else might have been involved in this scheme. Rosa couldn't possibly be doing this all alone; that was for certain. Was she in with a couple of criminals who had done this before? Did she have her family helping her, or were they truly innocent victims of her schemes too? Of course, when there's crime in Mexico, the authorities are as suspect as anyone else!

They have several forms of law enforcement in Mexico. There's the preventative police, the Rurals. They are like the country police. They work in the very hidden areas of the countryside. Then there's the *Federales*, who are similar to the highway patrolmen here in the United States. They take care of the roads and various other crimes around the country. They have the DER—their equivalent to our FBI. And, finally, they have customs officials who check the goods coming in and out of the country. There are a few more, but those are the main officials that business people and travelers need to be concerned with when crossing the border.

It's common knowledge in Mexico that, given the money, you can buy your way out of the worst of situations, including kidnapping, murder, armed robbery, rape and just about any other heinous crime imaginable. If fact, there is a saying in Mexico, *"Con dinero baila el perro."* The translation doesn't do it justice, but it means, "The dog dances with the money." God knows, I would have loved to see some dancing dogs just about that time of my kidnapping!

After the discussions had come to an end and the authorities and Keith had exhausted all the possibilities they could think of, my son and Maria returned to the outpost in McAllen. On the drive back, Keith was angry. When he exited the car, he screamed at the closest agent next to him, "What the hell are you guys doing? We are supposed to be here undercover! Who the hell is following her around?" The whole thing had overwhelmed him, and he had to let off the tension before going back home to face his mother. There was no other way but to let loose with it right then. He had been so under control until now; but after his conversation with Rosa, he was certain they had done something to screw things up. Now the Mexican authorities knew something. He didn't trust them at all. Even if they were on my side, Keith didn't trust that they were as covert as the FBI would be, nor would they be as adept at surveillance.

After that, the agents would often make Keith go outside the trailer they had previously set up as a second headquarters when they were discussing plans. It was in the trailer that the reality of the situation was discussed by the FBI—such as the unlikely possibility that this poor guy was getting out of Mexico alive, and if he did, would he be in such bad shape he would have rather not been saved. It was during these extremely frank conversations that the FBI feared Keith was too close to the situation and was getting too hotheaded to understand what their plans were. Maybe they were right. It really frustrated him, especially after he had been so involved. If all hell broke loose, Keith felt he was ultimately responsible for my safe return.

* * *

I felt Sunday melt away into Monday morning. There was that fucking rooster again. I would have preferred to sleep this horror away. The pain in my lower back hurt me so badly, I imagine it felt like a woman experiencing labor pains with a 40-pound baby. My lips were cracked and tasted of salt and blood most of the time. My tongue was swollen to twice its size, making it extremely difficult for me to swallow. Now, I often choked on nothing but fear and deprivation, and once I started coughing, I could not readily stop myself until I threw up a minute amount of spittle, and lining from my stomach. My head felt like the top of an aspirin bottle—dry, clogged, cottony!

The sounds of children heading to school filled my ears. I remembered the old days when Corinne sent our own kids off to school. They were such happy children. Did those outside school-hop and laugh as my children had, or did the poverty beat them down just as my captors did me? How could I be sitting right in the middle of this very busy neighborhood and no one notice a thing? I guess this sort of thing went on in the United States as well. You'd hear all the time about a serial killer who kept his victims in the basement or buried them in his backyard, and the cops would be none the wiser until years later. Would that be my case? Would they bury me somewhere in the backyard and nobody discover the body? Would my once happy kids be left to wonder what ever happened to their dad? What's wrong with people, anyway? This wasn't how God intended things to be! I never gave it much thought before, but I was one of the people going about my merry business while others may have been suffering!

I wondered whose house this was, and where they were while it was being used for this evilness? Did they know? Were they involved? Or, were they simply on a trip—soon to return and find their home invaded by bad men? The more I listened and the more voices I heard, the more I was

Terror In Mexico:
The Kidnapping of Ken Krusensterna

convinced that it took a good deal of people to pull something like this off. I mean, somebody had to bring in the groceries, they had to have a guard for the inside and outside of the house—perhaps even for the front and back of the house. They had to have someone who could contact my family while I was being watched. Lots of people—lots of people!

What about their families? Did their wives and children think they were out working a 9-5 job? Did they run to them looking for treats in their pockets and warm hugs or twirls around in the air? Somehow, I didn't picture the same men holding me captive as strong, reliable family men. It was obvious that the only ones they cared about were themselves, and the only thing that meant anything to them was money. They had no respect for human life, for dignity, for the human spirit!

"Drink!" I felt a small paper cup shoved to my lips. I thankfully inhaled the miniscule amount of water they offered me. Screw the admonishments of "don't drink the water." I would have gladly swallowed buckets of bacteria-ridden water by then. For a brief second, I allowed it to linger about my mouth, rehydrating the parched and cracked skin that must have no longer looked like lips, but rather like large, swollen, segmented worms circling my mouth. Painfully, I swallowed and was sorry to feel the last of it trickle down my throat. I was aware of every inch that the water passed on its way to my stomach. I prayed there would be another cup right away, but they apparently felt that was enough.

Okay, I was at least grateful I could keep it down. By then, even the water seemed to irritate my insides. Just before I could congratulate myself on my cast-iron stomach, here came the cook! What the devil that woman conjured up in the kitchen was beyond my imagination, but whatever it was it smelt foul, old, used, sour and greasy. Maybe those eating her terrible cooking were being as tortured as I was to be deprived of it! I had to concentrate to keep from throwing up by saying over and over in my mind, "Breathe! Don't throw up! Breathe! Settle!"

Mexican soap operas blared across the television nearest me as I tried to mentally scratch the increasing number of large welts from the attacking mosquitoes. It was times like these that I was convinced I had actually already died and gone to hell—a hell where the bugs were Boeings, nobody could understand me, my body was burning up, and I was deprived of all pleasure. What else could hell hold for me? Again, I tried to croak out a few words: "*Hombre*, problem?"

"No money. Family—no money."

"Why?"

"Tomorrow, no money, boom!" I got the clear meaning of that one. I decided not to ask that again. At least for a while.

Not far away, Otillio and Ron Coronado, the Zenith representative with whom I also had a good relationship, were on a mission. They had decided to try and locate my car to see if there might be any clues to my disappearance. They went back to the rental place and talked to the leasing salesperson.

"Are you sure it was a blue Taurus?" Otillio asked.

"Let me check one more time," she said. Ron and Otillio waited impatiently. "Oh, wait a minute. That car's been returned."

Terror In Mexico:
The Kidnapping of Ken Krusensterna

"What?" Ron and Otillio said, simultaneously.

"Yes, that car is back here."

"So, my friend doesn't have a car leased to him still?"

"Well, yes, we're still charging his card. Let me see if anyone knows why." The two men were confused. Would the kidnappers have had the heart or the balls to bring in the car? It didn't make sense. The screw up had to be here. It was. The agent came back. "It seems that your friend's car was blocked in when he went to get it, so one of our agents just let him take another car and forgot to make a notation."

"Well, can you tell us what kind of car that one was?"

"It was also a Taurus, but this one was maroon." Now they had a completely different color to look for, and they were angry about the amount of time wasted searching for the wrong car. The simple mistakes of the rental place and the hotel could have cost me my life.

Back across the border they went. Up and down the streets of Reynosa, in the back of shopping centers and grocery stores they searched. It was frustrating, but Otillio at last felt like he was accomplishing something in his attempts to locate the car and me. The two looked everywhere they could think of to look. Finally, on a stretch of road near a hospital, they spotted my car. They referred to the license number the agent had given them, and it matched. It was still locked as they peered inside, and it seemed to be in fairly good condition. Otillio could see that my belongings were still inside; at least the ones the kidnappers hadn't removed—like my hanging bag. They didn't disturb the evidence; they just left it and notified Keith that the car had been located with all my stuff inside. By the next day, it had been vandalized, gutted, and all the windows smashed. My hanging bag was long gone as well as my overnight bag and briefcase.

I knew it was Monday from my reference point of football the night before. Like a schoolboy, I was almost excited at the prospect of hearing Monday Night Football! Back in Dallas, Deanne, Corinne and Beth still waited for news. They had the drill down by now, especially Deanne. Phone would ring; recorder would turn on; she'd take a deep breath and say, "Hello." They were developing a routine with the FBI agents who stayed around the clock. They would eat together, talk some and worry a lot. Their minutes passed like days.

At the FBI outpost, Deanne waited for the call with Maria by her side ready to interpret if necessary. When the phone finally did ring, everybody jumped. Deanne's nerves were so shot, they decided it was best for Maria to answer the calls. They were confident that Rosa had informed her little gang of Maria's identity, so it was okay for her to answer. On the second ring Maria picked up the phone, saying hello in Spanish. The rest of the conversation continued in Spanish.

"Who is this?" came a very monotone voice.

"My name is Maria."

"What connection do you have to Ken?"

"I am a family friend, but I speak Spanish. The family asked for my help since there is a language barrier."

"Do they have the money?"

"They are going to need more time," Maria pleaded, as if she were asking a favor from a boss. She made sure to sound as if she were a bit unsure of herself, afraid of the caller.

"Why?" he demanded.

"Ken's family doesn't have that kind of money sitting in a checking account somewhere. It may take a day or so to raise it."

"I don't understand that. Can the son get the money?"

"Yes," Maria said, "but you have to understand. It's not like it is in the movies. People in the United States don't keep large sums of cash in a hidden safe behind a picture. Most people have their money tied up in Certificates of Deposits or other investments. They can't get their hands on huge amounts that quickly." Her answer seemed to pacify the man.

"Okay. You have until Wednesday; I'll call back then." He hung up the phone and Maria looked at the agent for news on the trace. He shook his head in the negative. It had been unsuccessful! Maria had stalled as long as she could without making the man suspicious; it just wasn't long enough. She did learn one thing about my kidnappers; something I too had thought. They weren't new to this. The man on the phone was a professional—he gave no inflection or emotion that might have given him away.

Looking at the bigger picture, it looked pretty bad for me right now. Thank God I didn't know the real story going on at home. Otillio had found my car, but no clues after the break-in. There was no word in Dallas and the FBI was unsuccessful in its trace. If I had known the real situation, my hopelessness may have turned to despair, and my will to live would have diminished to the size of a pea. For the moment, though, my circumstances had greatly improved with the little trickle of water they had just given me and the joy of not being beaten or battered about for at least an hour or more!

CHAPTER NINE
Day Nine

"**J**ust shoot me you son-of-a-bitch!"

On the ninth day, my hope of escape was really beginning to wane, and my mind was more distracted with thoughts of death than anything else. I became preoccupied with my preferred method of dying, which I planned out to the last detail. Most of all, I hated the thought of dying at the hands of these bastards. If it were my destiny to be in this chair much longer, I would just as soon they took me out now.

About the time I'd think myself resigned to death, I'd discover a glimmer of hope somewhere deep inside. Sometimes it came disguised in the form of worry—worry that my captors might get caught and refuse to tell where I was being held. I'd be abandoned, all alone, left to die of dehydration, boredom or something far worse. When I really got creative, I'd worry that my body would be ravaged by one of the many mangy animals that searched the garbage-filled streets at night for random tidbits of food. I was sure they weren't too proud to pick on the human variety, so I prayed my death would come by gun—quick and painless!

"Just shoot me you sons-of-bitches!" The words kept running through my mind, but, as I look back on it now, they were probably the fuel my mind needed to carry my weakened body through to the next hour, the next day, the next eternity it seemed! I took comfort in the worry. As long as I was worrying, I knew there was still some vestige of hope, some life left in them there bones of mine.

A bullet to the head was so much more humane than this. Why couldn't they just put me out of my misery? At least they wouldn't have to smell me anymore, or perhaps they were able to ignore the sourness of my sweating body and the stench of my flailing health as much as they ignored the voice within themselves that warned them this whole thing was wrong. No man deserved this, least of all a stranger who had never harmed them.

It occurred to me that I was once a hunter, yet now I was experiencing what it felt like to be on the other side of the gun. I was now the hunted, the trapped, the dying. In all my hunting trips, I had never thought of myself as cruel, but now I questioned what had once been one of my favorite sports. How could I have looked into the eyes of the innocent and taken their life? If I could do that with little awareness of loss or taken into consideration their feelings of helpless defeat at the hands of the conqueror, why did it surprise me that these men did the same? "No, no," I thought to myself, becoming agitated at the thought of us being more alike than we were different!

There went the fucking rooster again. It wasn't enough that he crowed once already this morning, but he had to give it another shot just to make sure I was good and awake. Thoughts of Colonel Sanders played through my head, and I fantasized about extra-crispy drumsticks; hot biscuits topped with melted butter and sticky honey; creamy, mashed potatoes smothered in steamy gravy. Talk about torture! My stomach growled its protest, and I had to discipline my thoughts, pulling them away from what I knew I couldn't have—food! I think, at that moment, I would have given my right arm for just one spoon full of food and a whole bottle of ice cold water.

Unlike my first morning awakening to this nightmare, I wasn't happy about survival—no longer elated because I had made it through another night. Now, all I wanted was for this to be over, one way or another. The rooster's cry always signaled a continuation to the hell I was going through. A very simple move to try for even the slightest relief to this incessant itching under my ass brought "Sex Man" to his feet in quick order.

"No move . . . boom!"

"My God, was that the only phrase this asshole could say?" I thought to myself. "Oh no," I giggled with just a touch of hysteria within, remembering he was proficient in moaning and grunting the words "*Rápido . . . rápido!*" in the throws of his so-called love making. He had another routine as well. Every day he would practice some sort of regular workout. With more grunting and groaning, I didn't know if he was gratifying himself, but then I recognized the pattern. He was doing sit-ups and push-ups. Much later when I saw the pictures of him, it was obvious that he must have worked out on a regular basis. Why the hell he didn't show that same sort of discipline in finding a job was beyond me. Of course, in his mind, he already had a job—the job of guarding me, and he took his work seriously.

Terror In Mexico:
The Kidnapping of Ken Krusensterna

Tap . . . tap . . . knock . . . knock! It was the morning signal that someone was entering. I smelled the cook before I heard her banging things around. I was like Pavlov's dog, conditioned to gag whenever the pans would bang and rattle in the kitchen. The gag reflex was simply in response to the disgusting smell of greasy food that was sure to follow within the hour after Cook had entered, if she decided not to have a sex break before breakfast!

Time for me to relax and think of what my family was doing right now and how they were planning my rescue. Those thoughts would surely keep the bile from rising in my throat and the pain of my irritated skin at bay. I had a pretty good idea that the family had contacted someone, because they had tried the cell phone. Besides, I was still alive, and these were not patient men willing to wait an eternity for my family to take action. We were all playing the waiting game, and I knew it must be almost as difficult for my family as it had been for me this past week. Damn, a whole week had passed. It's amazing how time stands still when you've nothing to do but focus on taking one breath after another to keep yourself from convulsing.

* * *

Closer to home, Keith had managed to stall Rosa with a promise to work on getting the money. She seemed placated by that and left with a new message for the kidnappers. Keith hated the sense he had that she was happy when hearing about the money. She was happy at the expense of the total devastation of our family. She was happy at the misery of others, and he knew she was in it just as deeply as those she blamed. How, I don't know, but Keith was able to remain calm and patient with Rosa's incriminating conversations. He listened and planned, waiting for his moment of revenge.

Even to his inexperienced eye, Keith knew that the more time they could buy without making the kidnappers angry, the better chance they had of finding me alive. The FBI and Keith spent the day devising a plan of attack from the trailer in McAllen, which served as headquarters. While all this went on inside those crowded quarters, my home in Dallas was also filling up with the strangers this sort of emergency attracts.

Of course, the girls had circled the wagons around Corinne, trying to reassure her things would work out, even though they doubted the truth of what they were saying with every passing day. Deanne left work immediately upon receiving the news of my kidnapping to stay with her mother at our home. Deanne was tough, but her job working with troubled juvenile delinquents at a last-chance boot camp hadn't prepared her for my kidnapping. Because of her job, Deanne had jumped to the early conclusion that I had been "jacked" by a bunch of gang-bangers. Apparently, the border towns were crawling with those types of kids, and she assumed I had been beaten up and left for dead in a back alley somewhere.

Wondering if she had done the right thing in calling the McAllen police to file a missing person's report, she rolled her actions around in her head over and over again. She beat herself up and constantly questioned the wisdom of her every move. The McAllen police had referred her to our local department, saying that's where she needed to file. Concerned about following all the right channels, she called the Grand Prairie Police Department and made another report. They soon called her back and referred her to the Bureau of Missing Persons in Austin. I can proudly say, I was now on file with more police departments than the ten most wanted!

Although all my kids are resilient, strong individuals, and Deanne is no different, her pinched expression and tightened neck muscles were beginning to signal her increasing tenseness. She just didn't know whom to trust. Here my captors were, making the impossible demands of $350,000, and she didn't know if honoring their demands would even bring me back alive.

Just a few weeks earlier, she had been talking to some friends whose father was in jail in Mexico. They had already sent over $100,000, and still no sign of Dad! Like Keith, Deanne was beginning to realize you trust no one! It doesn't matter if they wear a dirty red bandanna or a freshly washed uniform; one could easily be as corrupt as the other. In times like these, even the strongest look for some sort of support, and Deanne's boss, Dr. Kessner, offered her some much needed comfort in the midst of our family crisis. Not only did she allow Deanne the time off, but she kept others from calling the house and disrupting the FBI systems they'd put in place. She was constantly offering Deanne advice and helpful numbers whenever asked, and most of all, she was a voice of normalcy from a past life Deanne barely remembered. Would life ever return to what it was? Would she ever be that carefree, helpful social worker again—the one willing to help the troubled, believing there was always a little good in people burdened by bad?

It was also a comfort having Beth in from Phoenix, even though she could be a loose cannon with her bouts of rowdy anger and her constant need to be given every bit of information that had been communicated before her arrival. Although the girls had fought like cat and dog as kids, they pulled together like warriors now. Sometimes they would sit outside and talk for hours, reminiscing about the good ol' days. Beth recalled the time her dog was killed by a speeding car, and I took her to Puppy Land to shop for a new addition to the family. She let the tears fall freely down her cheeks as she remembered my laughter at her choice of hounds; she picked the most pitiful one in the bunch to take home. There was no question but that Beth's compassion would cause her to pick the dog closest to the chair on death row to save and make happy. That's my Beth, tough on the outside and pretty much a marshmallow on the inside!

Deanne informed Beth of their brother's conversation with Rosa and of her claims that my first words to the captors had been "Don't hurt me . . . don't hurt me! I have money! I can pay!" They both looked at one another, saying the same word aloud: "Bullshit!" They knew me better than that. It was almost comical to think that any Krusensterna might utter those words, much less their dad. Beth nodded her agreement when Deanne commented that every last one of us would fight for our freedom. My girls know me, and as they puffed away on one cigarette after another, they discussed the inconsistencies of Rosa's story and the things that just didn't make sense to them.

Terror In Mexico:
The Kidnapping of Ken Krusensterna

They had quite a past together. As kids, they too had inherited the Krusensterna character traits of stubbornness and persistence, along with a little from their mother as well. Although they were quick to anger one another, nobody dared to harm a hair on one of their heads without the fear of drawing Krusensterna wrath. It was fine for them to beat the hell out of each other, but, by God, if somebody else bared arms, there'd be hell to pay. Little did the kidnappers know, they had slim to no chance to defeat us—or so we all hoped!

I can picture the girls, grown women, sitting there in front of the house plotting their assault on Mexico. I'll have to admit, it was difficult to contain my laughter as I was recovering in the hospital, when I heard the antics of these two. They shared with me their plan of going to the armory to get a Bradley Tank and drive it right up to Rosa's house. The only arguments they were having was whether to use a 9mm or an AK47. There was no shame on their faces when sharing these stories with me in the hospital, only regret that they were helpless in carrying them out. After all, they are passionate women, and the bad guys had their dad!

Of course, when the discussions outside the house got too heated, and they felt fired up to go invade Mexico, there were always more distractions going on inside the house. FBI agents had pretty much invaded. It started out with just two agents and soon grew to five. They would question the girls in different ways, using different tactics, but it all boiled down to the same thing—information they could get that might give them a clue as to how to plan a successful rescue.

They were skilled interrogators. Few of them repeated questions the others had already posed. One question might just trigger information they hadn't previously heard. Actually, their level of communication and expertise was highly competent, and the girls have often said since then that the FBI's professionalism and dedication to get me home was incredible. Deanne especially remembers an agent named Doug. He had a natural way about him that served to calm her ragged nerves and get her thinking positively. Doug allowed her to vent without judgment, knowing that it was necessary for her to get the anger out in order to keep her from imploding. Few people think of the human side of FBI agents, but, in our case, we saw many examples of their kindness and compassion.

Beth, on the other hand, was through with empty conversations. All she wanted to do was ACT! If she thought it would have done any good, I believe she would have traveled to Reynosa to run up and down the streets, yell my name and offer the $350,000 ransom money to the first one who found me. The worst thing for Beth was her feelings of helplessness. Unlike Deanne, she'd never been one to analyze a situation—it was more in her nature to do now and apologize later.

It was becoming increasingly difficult to cover with the neighbors, trying to explain away the half a dozen cars in the drive and the suited men coming in and out all day, so everybody stopped trying. For the first time, the Krusensterna family became recluses; rarely leaving the house except for essentials—like cigarettes, alcohol to numb the pain, and the peace of mind a short absence could bring.

Terror In Mexico:
The Kidnapping of Ken Krusensterna

It's incredulous how Murphy's Law can be hard at work even in the middle of a life-threatening crisis. Deanne picked up the phone to make a call, and her heart skipped a beat.

"What the hell? The lines dead!" she said to nobody in particular. She placed it back on its cradle in the hope that perhaps it had accidentally been knocked off the hook. She lifted the phone again, but still no dial tone. Next, she ran to grab her cell phone, only to find it had a dead battery rendering it inoperable. Her hands shaking, she ran to her car to plug it in for a battery boost. Mercifully, it worked, and she reached customer service at the phone company.

"You've got to help us—our phone line's dead!" she shouted into the receiver.

As Murphy's Law would have it, there was an old business account in my name that hadn't been paid, for some unexplainable reason. The result was the phone company had picked this time to shut off our service.

Deanne continued with her tirade, screaming at the operator, "You don't understand. I have to get this phone turned back on, immediately."

The operator gave a little perfunctory click and hiss, responding with, "You'll need to pay the bill, first, ma'am!"

"God damn it; I'll pay whatever is due, just get my phone back on. My father has been kidnapped, and we're waiting on a call from the kidnappers regarding the ransom."

"Just a minute, please."

Deanne suspected she sounded like another crazy caller to the operator, but her first concern was to get phone service, and get it fast. Within a few seconds, the woman returned to the line, saying, "It'll be back on in about 30 minutes. Here's where you can go to pay the amount owed."

Barely able to listen to the operator's directions, Deanne flew to the nearest pay station. She immediately drove over, and as luck would have it, Murphy had his way again. The pay station was located at the Fiesta Market, a store frequented almost exclusively by Hispanics. Although Deanne had not been prejudice in the past, she gave thought that day to blasting every brown body in that market to kingdom come. It's easy to see why she was filled with such loathing for the entire race, so angry, in fact, that she could barely find the sign that read "*Teléfono* payments, *aquí.*" The sign had once read "Telephone payments, here" but someone had scratched out the first and last word of English and rewrote them in Spanish. She paid the money, and quickly exited the store before she too ended up in chains.

Back home, everybody was instructed to follow the system. There were two phones in the house and both had recorders attached to them. They were about the same size and shape as a Walkman tape player and had two lines running from the phone and headset. When the phone rang, Deanne would get in place to pick it up along with an agent. He'd click on the tape recorder, and she'd pick up the phone. If the caller was a family member or a friend, she'd give him a "thumbs-up" and he'd turn off the recorder. It was the same old routine for hours on end. The phone would ring, and everybody in the house would jump out of their skins.

What made it worse for them all is when some idiots would call soliciting or wanting some other meaningless conversation. One such person was a man from this credit card company. Wanting to complete some unfinished business with my company and convinced his persistence would soon pay off by getting to talk to the man in charge, he just kept calling and calling. Four and five times a day the little pisser would be on the phone. Little did he know that the man in charge at that time was an FBI agent, and his calls were creating havoc with my family. Finally, Deanne could hold back her frustrations no longer, and the poor fellow got blasted by one more irate, hysterical female on the other end of the line. I believe the conversation went something like this: "Look mister, my dad will call you as soon as he gets home. If you call this house one more time asshole, I'll come through this line—and then we're both going to have one huge, fucking problem!"

By this time, Deanne had worked up quite a phone list of possible contacts. She had collected Otillio's numbers, both at home and the office in Mexico. It was only a matter of time before she added my Reynosa secretary to the list. She had Rosa's numbers; and, let me tell you, it took the strength of Hercules to keep her from calling that woman from time to time. I thanked God as I lay in my hospital bed that Beth didn't have Rosa's number all that time. I'm sure it would have been Rosa recovering in the hospital bed if that had been the case.

* * *

Back in the hellhole, time was clicking by—one long stream of endless time. I was fading in and out of consciousness and getting weaker with each passing day. I sensed the presence of another person then felt them touch something gross to my lips. Within a matter of seconds, I had identified the taste. Banana! Someone was trying to cram a banana between my pursed lips. I could be thankful it wasn't some of the toxins being whipped up in the kitchen, but its squishy texture and probably bruised exterior did little to stimulate my appetite.

My jaws refused to work as I tried to keep myself from choking. After about three bites I had to stop before my stomach nixed the idea of accepting this intrusion all together. Then they gave me my token sip of water. It was like a trickling rain hitting dry, cracking clods of dirt.

About the time the moisture had soaked in, my mind began to play tricks on me. Far off in the distance, I saw this beautifully brilliant light, beckoning me to walk toward it. As I traveled the tunnel of flashing colors, I somehow felt comforted the closer I got to the light. It occurred to me that I had heard about phenomenons like this happening to people who had a near-death experience, and I began to wonder if this was it for me. If so, it was certainly an improvement over that despicable chair and my hateful captors.

Wow, the colors, the lights—so bright—so beautiful! I felt no pain, no fear and no discomfort as I got closer and closer to the light. I wanted to stay, so I waited for somebody to greet me and promise me everything was going to be okay for my family if I left them behind. That isn't exactly what happened, though. Suddenly, I was sucked back through the colorful tunnel and down into the chair. I saw no guardian angels and no dead family member reaching to take me to the other side. Instead it was a swift, harsh return to reality.

Terror In Mexico:
The Kidnapping of Ken Krusensterna

Having had a short respite, the pain now was excruciating. My head rolled forward so violently that "Sex Man" came to check my pulse. I had quit trying to plead my case, quit trying to fight, and most of all, quit expecting a rescue around every corner. Now all I wanted was for the pain to stop. I wanted to go back to the light and get out of these chains. I guess "Sex Man" wanted his money more than I wanted my death, because he kept slapping me into consciousness, ignoring my moans of protest.

I think, even "Sex Man" worried about me that night—afraid that I might die and he'd have a 200-pound lump on his hands with no money to show for his efforts. I do believe he even skipped his nightly romp that evening, needing to concentrate on keeping me conscious and alive. Did the asshole think to give me another glass of water or a few mouthfuls of food? Absolutely not! Those acts of kindness were beyond him. Instead, he threatened me with the same old, tired phrases and repeatedly slapped my face until it too was numb from his stinging abuse.

The night passed like every other had that week, and my hope died a little more with my bodily functions. Having nothing left over that my body wasn't attempting to use in order to save my life, I rarely went to the bathroom on myself anymore. I was beginning to understand the fact that "the man in black" would soon become my closest companion as I entered through death's door, but I somehow couldn't muster up enough energy to care anymore. My last conscious thoughts that evening weren't of hate or retribution, revenge or escape; instead, I thought how lucky it would be for all of us if I just died in my sleep!

CHAPTER TEN
Day Ten or Was It Day Eleven?

Whoever would have thought that I would consider this day just another routine one to follow the others that had passed in my kidnapping? It was the same smells, sounds and activities of the days before, with the only difference being that my senses were dulled to the intensity of the moment. I had experienced a rough night—such horrible, uncontrollable shaking that I thought the chair I was chained to would surely fall apart. Again my guard threw the dirty piece of carpet over me, perhaps to stop my teeth from chattering a rhythm to beat the band.

There were times that I could not distinguish my thoughts or hopes from my reality; they tended to be just one big blur. The most frightening thing now was that I could feel my body shutting down, and I knew my days were numbered. If I weren't rescued soon, my family could save themselves the money. Who knew, at this point it might already be too late to save my ass.

With the increasing heat came the bug brigade and the overpowering need to scratch off my outer layer. Fear didn't stop my movements anymore, but they were so slight they were hardly noticeable. Yep, my movements went unnoticed today, especially on this morning with all the increased excitement and the heightened mood of my kidnappers. For once, they were all in an "up" mood, and there was an air or expectancy in the room. The feeling of anticipation served to bolster my mental well-being if not my physical strength but, with that, my fear returned. What was to happen that would make today different from all the others?

"Today, *señor*, *mucho* money!"

"Family?" I asked.

"*Sí*! *Mucho* money, *señor*."

"Will I be released?" I tried to ask, knowing, full well, I could not trust the response to that question. If it were "yes," who could believe them? If it were "no," who wanted to believe them?

"Ssshhh! Boom!" they laughed, pointing the gun in my cheek then moving it just and few inches from my face from the sound of it and firing it into the ceiling.

Doesn't anybody hear those shots and wonder what the hell is going on inside this shack? Doesn't anybody in this shitty place have any compassion? I was growing to hate the sound of that gun, and I wondered if I would be released from this fucking chair only to have the pelted ceiling collapse on me. Although their mood was jovial, mine was one of trepidation.

Unbelievably, my mind was now wide awake. Had they received the ransom? Would I be going home soon? Or, would I have suffered all this time to be shot and dumped in a river somewhere? I was one huge bundle of nerves; I would have said nervous energy, but energy had nothing to do with the way I was feeling. What did all their excitement mean? Now that my mind was more alert, my body began

Chapter Ten:
Day Ten or Was It Day Eleven?

following its lead. I once again went through any plans I had previously made for escape, but even I doubted whether my body was up for busting out of the chair and running out the door and through the streets naked. I doubted whether the neighbors were ready for such a sight either.

If I could only see what I was up against, I'd know the answers to these questions. I checked my mental calendar, which was difficult when one day overlapped another in this world of depressing sameness. By my calculations, it had to be about Wednesday, or was it Thursday? Even if it was only Wednesday, I'd been here well over a week. Ten or eleven days as best I could tell. How had I survived, or more importantly, how would I continue to survive if this was not to be my last day in captivity?

The smell of money attracted more and more of the devils, and they began to arrive by what sounded like truck loads of people coming to a reunion during old home week. The foreign chatter was nerve-racking, and the blaring televisions and smell of greasy food was almost more than I could take. It was like having a party in your honor, only you show up naked, sick and in a very foul mood. Some of the voices I could hear sounded happy, some sounded drunk, and some sounded pissed at all the commotion. Those alarmed me the most. I feared their anger now that I felt so close to getting out of this thing.

* * *

I was right on one account—it was Wednesday. It had slipped my mind at the time, but that particular Wednesday was Veteran's Day, which was both good and bad. Bad because it meant another day my family could not get the money and another day I had to remain in that God awful chair. It was a good day, however, for the FBI, because it gave them another excuse to stall and plan.

The FBI agents were in our back pocket, that's for sure, but they were not eager partners to the fiasco. It would seem that many, actually most, of the kidnappings perpetrated in Mexico on American citizens are drug related. So, once they had determined the kidnapping was for real, they set out to do some extensive background checking on me. They investigated my company down there; they ran checks on all my former companies and did a fairly thorough check on me, personally. Now, I'm no "Snow White," but I'm no "Dopey" either. I knew better than to run things in my companies under the table, and it probably saved my life.

The FBI further questioned Deanne about all my past IRS dealings and my credit situation. They had to make sure that Ken Krusensterna deserved their attentions. Thank God I led a legitimate life, otherwise I'd have been coyote fodder. After all their investigations, they finally decided my ass was worth risking theirs for, and they went to work full steam ahead.

The extent of the Grand Prairie Police Department's investigations in the filed missing person's report was to call everyday to see if I'd shown up. Of course, the phone calls sent everybody in the room through the roof, but the family was instructed by the FBI to avoid giving any information to the local police to insure there would be no leaks. I still can't imagine the raw nerves of the girls and Corinne as they jumped each time the shrill of the phone signaled a possible contact, only to be disappointed that it was some unknowing caller caught in the web of this emergency.

No other police department ever really did an active search for me, convinced I would show up floating face down in the river somewhere or curled in a fetal position in the back streets of Dallas' own poor side of town. Most are familiar with those parts of town; you know the "shoot-'em-and-watch-them-rot" district every city has where life exists in 3D—depression, drugs and death! All the police department wanted to do was locate my body so they could scratch me off their list and move on to the next poor soul depending on its help to make the difference between a life-and-death situation. With so many missing children these days, the urgency to find an older adult just isn't that strong. After all, there could be so many other reasons for an adult's disappearance. With no crime scene and no clues, the police move on to search out hotter trails promising more rewards for their efforts.

What was surprising to the family was that the FBI had strongly suggested withholding information from the local police for fear of media leaks or other trouble that usually accompanied such exploits. The girls were hanging on, but just barely. Deanne was so afraid for Corinne's health that she soon assumed the parental role. She'd tell her mother to take a nap and get her rest, and Corinne's physical weaknesses required her to take another pill and try to get just 30 minutes of uninterrupted sleep. Her doctors had no idea they'd have to refuse to let her answer her phone as part of her recovery instructions, but it had come to that.

When Corinne rose above the affects of her medication, she would repeatedly ask to talk to Keith, but he and Deanne had agreed that they wouldn't tell her much—just that everything was going along as planned and that I'd soon be home. This placated her, but Beth was another story. Beneath the surface of her hazed condition, Corinne never thought I wouldn't be coming home. On the flip side, Beth wanted to know why I wasn't home already! What was the holdup? Why weren't Deanne and Keith telling the whole story? At the time, they thought they were protecting both Beth and me, but withholding information was tough on Beth. It was over this very issue that Beth and Deanne got into a gigantic altercation. Seeing that there was just that one disagreement between them in over a week, I'd say that was a record for the girls.

* * *

Things were heating up down in Mexico as well. Rosa had called Otillio on his cell phone, asking, "Why aren't they doing anything, Otillio?"

"I don't know anything about what's going on," he answered, trying to avoid raising her anger and suspicions.

"What should I do?" she'd plead. The nerve of the bitch asking my friend and manager for advice on proper kidnapping etiquette! There was no getting around it—she had the gonads of a prize bull!

"I am not involved here, Rosa. No one has told me anything."

Chapter Ten:
Day Ten or Was It Day Eleven?

"Do you think they have the police involved?" she asked, trying to milk Otillio for information he wasn't willing to give or didn't know.

"I don't know. I'm sure they don't if Ken's life is at stake."

"Well, I went to church, and there was someone following me; I'm sure of it. Please Otillio, what do you know?"

"It's like I told you; I don't know anything."

"I need for you to call Keith for me."

"I will not do that! It's not my place, Rosa."

"Can you call and find out, Otillio?" she'd continue as if not hearing his first response.

"Rosa, I'm not going to do anything else. I am not involved in this case in any way. I want to stay out of things." And, that was it! Otillio was tired and frightened for his family. With each passing day that I wasn't found, Otillio became a prisoner as well, prisoner to his fears that I would never be found and that he and Ron might be blamed for my death. He continued to move his family around from one friend or relative's home to another, never going anywhere without the protection of one of his male cousins. It was a miserable time for Otillio, and I am sorry for the pain brought to him and his family. In a way, they too had been kidnapped.

Rosa had still not contacted Keith, and he feared the repeated stalls had costs me my life. He was visibly shaken when he finally got to speak with her but conscious not to ruffle her tail feathers. The call was recorded, and Keith had rehearsed his part over and over. He concentrated on keeping his voice calm and non-threatening with her.

Terror In Mexico:
The Kidnapping of Ken Krusensterna

"Do you have the money?"

"We've hit a snag, Rosa. The money just got transferred last night and today is a holiday."

"What does that mean?" Rosa asked, a hint of impatience found in her question.

"Our banks are closed here on national holidays."

"Um . . . when should I tell them that you'll have the money?" she continued to push for the exchange, trying to sound nonchalant.

"I'll have it tomorrow. Call me then."

"I will do that," she replied. Keith hung up, taking comfort in the reassurances of the FBI that he had played his part well. They were impressed with his calm, organized demeanor. My heart gets full every time I think of the hardships that kid was asked to overcome. Only 21 years old and dealing with the weight of the world; that's a heavy burden for anybody to carry; but coupled with the inexperience of youth, it's a wonder Keith didn't crack under the pressure. Instead, he kept telling Deanne that when all of this was over, he was going home. By home, Keith meant home to Wisconsin, where life was simpler and decisions weren't life-and-death.

Deanne marveled at Keith's strength, saying, "You have to do what makes you happy. You can't live for someone else, and if that's where you want to be, then go!"

Because the kidnappers were again using my cell phone, it was next to impossible for the FBI to clearly trace the calls. Tops on their task list was to get the kidnappers to use "land" phones. As the situations changed and progress was made or lost, Keith was briefed on what to say and do.

He listened well, rarely making a mistake. In fact, he never, as far as I know, showed one ounce of weakness to the enemy.

No matter how competent the family, the FBI and the local and Mexican police were, something was going to have to break soon, or I was going to die. When you are certain that death is imminent, it is amazing the calming affect that can have. All the animated voices of my captors, all the television noise, all the slaps and abuse—nothing phased me anymore. For the first time since my kidnapping, I felt invincible. They couldn't hurt me!

Over the voices and noise, I heard another sound, a purer sound—clean fresh rain was soaking into my mind and clearing away the clouds. Water! I would have loved, at that moment, to go out into the street stark-raving naked and just stand beneath its cleansing force, open my mouth and let it fill me from head to toe. Rain! What a great sound: rain hitting the hardened roof of the house, trickling down the sides of the windows. I thought about the weather in Dallas, remembering how welcoming it was this time of year.

Next my thoughts took me to Thanksgiving, and I wondered if my family would have much to be thankful for this year. Of course, my next logical thoughts were of succulent, roasted turkey, stuffed to the max with moist homemade dressing and an apple in its belly to add just the right touch of flavor. Hell, I'd have been happy for just the apple right about then. Nothing to do, but think about the simple pleasures of life and wait for whatever was to happen next.

I fell asleep that night knowing that the night would fade to the morning, and hell week would start all over again,

Terror In Mexico:
The Kidnapping of Ken Krusensterna

but I simply didn't care any longer. God must certainly have plans for me if he had kept my body going during all their abuse. It would be too bad if I had gone through all this only to die in the end. Not fair—I had earned my freedom! I wanted this to be over so badly that now I didn't really care how it ended—just so it did!

I was totally unaware of the political activities going on behind the scenes, and, thank God, so did my captors. I owe part of my survival to the timing of those politics. The Mexican Government had been under a lot of pressure to stop this sort of thing from happening. Americans provided a great deal of the country's revenue, and if U.S. businessmen and women and recreational travelers didn't feel safe, "*mucho denaros*" would be lost to the Mexican people and their government.

By then, even Janet Reno had gotten involved in my case by giving the go ahead to send up a spy plane as soon as a trace was confirmed. I know; it really sounds like 007 material, but this is the scene that was being played out for my release. I didn't even have to be a diplomat, a politician, or friend to a wealthy tycoon. Our government was just as willing to help one lone American, and I can't thank them enough for their persistent belief in the importance of rescuing one of their own.

Once they knew where I was being held, the plane could go overhead, and with their infrared lasers search through house after house to pinpoint movements and the activities of occupants living there. *El Presidente* didn't have much choice but to allow the plane to fly over Mexican airspace; the FBI and American government were very firm with their demands.

Chapter Ten:
Day Ten or Was It Day Eleven?

Much later, I heard that I was due to be shot that day if news of the money wasn't positive. If another message came back with no hope of recovering any money, they intended to kill me that day. Fortunately, the call to Rosa came just in time.

"Rosa, I have the money," Keith told her, even though all the money wasn't there. For some reason, Keith felt he must make his move now—no time to wait for additional funds.

"Where should we meet?" she asked.

"How about the same hotel where we met before," Keith answered.

"Why do I have to come over there?" she pouted, almost ready to stomp her foot at the inconvenience "poor little rich boy" Keith was dishing out. "Why?"

"Because, I don't really know how to get this much money across the border."

"Alright then, I'll meet you at the hotel." That was ideal because it had been set up already for taping and surveillance. In truth, Keith had only been able to raise half the money and did not know where the rest was to come from. He hoped they wouldn't need it. Between my business partner, Fred, and my family, they had about $175,000 all stacked neatly into an unassuming briefcase. The agents and Keith headed out for the hotel in plenty of time to stage the room for Rosa's arrival.

Keith poised himself in the room and waited for her knock. She was there right on time. "Is that you, Rosa?" Keith asked through the door.

"Yes!"

"Come on in," he invited, even though he felt more like slamming the door right in her face.

"You said that you had the money!" she immediately voiced her concerns and was unable to contain her excitement long enough for small talk.

"I do. At least half of it!"

"What? When do you get the rest?"

"It shouldn't be any later than tomorrow; I just wanted to let them know that I was trying to get the cash. This is a lot of money—it just isn't that easy!" He opened the case and showed her the money. There was no mistaking the gleam in her eyes. They lighted up like firecrackers on the Fourth of July. The sight of so much money was obviously making her forget her affected sorrow and fear. She reached to take the money from Keith, and he had to purposefully unball his fist as her fingers brushed his hand.

"Whoa! Not so fast! My family and I will not turn over this money until we know that Dad is still alive."

"How do I have them do that?" she asked, irritated as she watched Keith close the briefcase and pull it away from her.

"He needs to call me at this number." It was a number that would not receive cellular calls. They had to get them to a phone that was traceable.

"When should I tell them to call?"

"I'll need time to get back to it," Keith said, not wanting to give her the impression that the number was in McAllen.

"And then, what do I do?"

"Then we make arrangements to meet again, and I will have all the money for you to take to the kidnappers." It was

Chapter Ten:
Day Ten or Was It Day Eleven?

Keith's hope and thought that they would call back that very night. He desperately wanted to hear from me—anything at all, just hear my voice. He wanted to hear my voice and confirm that all this effort wasn't in vain. For the first time since early childhood, Keith needed his father.

He watched as she walked out the door. There was such a contrast to the crying young woman he had seen during their first meeting. With a bounce in her step and a confidence in her demeanor, she looked almost happy. Why shouldn't she? She was about to become a very wealthy young Mexican woman.

We assumed that she would return to her home and relay the message to the kidnappers. They would be anxious to get their hands on the money and get rid of me. They probably discussed into the night how to go about getting me to a phone so they could collect their money. I'm sure that somewhere in those lengthy discussions they devised a plan. It wasn't difficult for me to know that something was about to take place and it definitely had to do with money because the excitement was high and so were they. The kidnappers felt certain, with the confirmation by Rosa, that the money was there and they were all going to be rich men! They drank their tequila and smoked their marijuana, celebrating like they'd won the lottery, except the prize was my life. I knew my family would do whatever it took to get me home. I could only hope the bastards would uphold their end of the bargain!

CHAPTER ELEVEN
Would Today be the Day?

It was a sick joke—God had some sense of humor, I'd say! How could I still be alive? I thought that every breath was going to be my last and then another would regretfully follow. I felt like a fish on a string, given just enough water to stay alive but left to lay there and suffer beside the lake still in sight of the water. Yep, I felt like a fish who would spend its last days watching its friends swimming and jumping in and out of the water. Finally, that fish, out of its element, simply gives up—stops the struggle for a life it really doesn't want to live! If I saw a fish like that, I'd at least have the decency to club it to death on a rock instead of letting it die slowly, with the hope someone would walk by and toss it back in the river just in the nick of time.

All along, during my days and days of being blindfolded, I had learned to develop a keen sense of hearing. But, hearing carried a private torture all its own. Often times I would hear one of my captors sitting out on the front porch with a neighbor just shootin' the shit, as if he hadn't a care in the world. Nobody knew there was a kidnapped American chained to a chair for almost two weeks now, wondering if somebody—anybody—would ever rescue him.

Chapter Eleven:
Would Today be the Day?

Like the morning before, on that morning, there came another knock at the door and more raised voices in the excitement of the moment. By now, I had learned not to get my hopes up. They had gotten excited before, and all that had happened was more disappointment, anger and a slam on my head, slap across my face or a wooden baton bounced off my chins for the trouble I'd supposedly caused. Then there would be silence—just like now.

The others left, and I was alone with my guard. About an hour passed. Then there came the window signal. Next thing I knew, things started happening quite quickly. I felt them lift the chains to release them. My heart seemed to be the only thing left in me with the energy to move, and it gave a sudden leap at the thought of freedom. Was I going home? They didn't seem too pissed off, and it was a proven fact it didn't take much disappointment to create that emotion in them! Maybe a deal had been negotiated for my release—I prayed that were true!

Very slowly I stood up, or leaned up I should say. I was weak as a newborn foal, all wobbly and unsure of myself. My back screamed out as it was stretched to an upright position. Muscles I had forgotten protested my every move! "God, the blood—it's killing me," my mind yelled its anger at the sudden pain, but nothing came from my dry throat except a squeaky, low moan. The blood continued to flow to parts of my atrophied muscles that had been as starved for blood as I had been for food, and they were letting me know about it. More blood, forcing its way through my veins, like an eighteen wheeler carrying an extra-wide load trying to squeeze through a rickety, wooden covered bridge built in the 1700s.

Terror In Mexico:
The Kidnapping of Ken Krusensterna

The path was too narrow, and the passage too worn out for the blood to rush its way through my body that fast!

I nearly passed out from the pain of newly circulated blood; then they directed me to walk. Where was I going? Before I could form the question on my parched lips, I heard water running in what sounded like a shower. Were they going to let me shower? They whacked me on the leg to indicate there was a step up into the water closet. I felt the cold blast of water hit my face, and for the first time in days I started to feel alive again and eager to suck in life's little pleasures.

The most difficult decision I'd had to make in a lifetime was that of whether to drink the water or let it run down my body. I tried my best to do a lot of both. There was no soap, but I was in no position to be picky. I felt things crusted on my body and stuck within every crevice and fold, but it was impossible to wash them off or out, whatever the case may be. When I ran my hand between my legs where the urine had gathered and burned through the skin, I flinched at its rawness and nerves afire with the torture of human touch.

"Move on Ken. Get your mind on the positive!" I thought, eager to luxuriate in the free-flowing water. I gulped a mouthful of water and washed it around from side to side then bloated my cheeks out in an attempt to rinse the slime from my teeth. The water swished around from side to side, coated my swollen tongue and cooled my reddened gums. I couldn't get enough down my throat without choking on its content.

All of this wonder lasted only a moment or two until they were shoving me out of the shower and herding me back into the other room. I would have given anything to have spent a full 30 minutes in there with shampoo, soap and a razor. Of course, I couldn't have promised that the razor would have been used on my beard! Then I felt a pain in my right arm, and I welcomed its presence. It was the arm I earlier believed had been severed, but they had not cut it off after all. Like the rest of my body, it had merely fallen asleep from the restricted circulation. Slowly, I headed back into that dreadful room. "God, don't let them put me back into that torturous chair," I pleaded, willing to make a deal with the devil since his kidnapping colleagues weren't listening. I thought I'd try talking to them one more time—catch them in a playful mood and see if I could discover their plans.

"*Señor*, doctor?"

"No doctor. *Mucho* money."

"Did you get my family?"

"*Sí, señor*. Your family . . . *mucho* money." And, that was it. I felt something get laid over my hands and realized it was the familiar material of my clothing. My heart was leaping. I had to be going home. Why else would they not want me to see them? Why else would they get me cleaned up and dressed? Surely they weren't just going to do that and then kill me. I tried to get my shirt on over the chains, but it wouldn't fit. They cut it so the chains could remain where they were. They weren't about to take any chances that I would escape.

After putting my shirt on, they realized that I couldn't get my pants on, either. One of them loaded a gun, made sure I heard the magazine click, and shoved it in my face, saying, "No move, boom."

Terror In Mexico:
The Kidnapping of Ken Krusensterna

I nodded my understanding. They slowly untied my legs and put a chain and padlock around my waist. I gingerly stepped into my pants, so unsteady that my focus became concentrated on lifting one leg then another. Finally came my loafers, once easy slip-ons but my now swollen feet refused them entry. They required the impossible from me—bending over. I was only able to slip in the front portions of my feet and have my heels rest of the folded backs of my shoes. Although I had no energy to bend over to secure my shoes, my body was now doubling over in pain. About the time I raised into a standing position, I realized just how loose feeling my clothing had become. My shirt hung from my shrunken shoulders, and my pants required assistance to keep them in place. I had lost more than forty pounds, but it was not a diet I'd recommend.

"No look . . . boom!" They started taking off my blindfolds. I couldn't believe I was actually going to see again. I positioned my eyes so they were peering straight ahead, so as not to threaten my captors. I needn't have bothered. The blindfold came off, and I involuntarily jerked and squinted at the pain. The light hitting my eyes was like a thousand knives jabbed bullseye on the center of my pupils. I couldn't see a thing and wondered why they had taken off my blindfold, but I was soon to get an answer to that question.

They cut out pieces of cloth and taped them over my eyes. It was a pretty shoddy job—a sharp contrast to the extreme professionalism they had shown to this point. Fearing for my life if the tape were to come off, I prayed my captors would not notice my increasing sight. That worry was needless as well. They placed sunglasses over my bandages hoping people on the street would not notice the patches on my eyes and suspect foul play. A dirty baseball cap completed my pitiful ensemble. I'm sure that was to cover my blood-encrusted scalp, which would have drawn attention in even the most oblivious of social circles.

Open and close—open and close! Over and over, I heard the door open and close as if someone were checking on movement outside. When they felt confident that all was clear, they guided me out. The short walk to the carport where the vehicle was waiting seemed like miles for my Jello-legs to travel. Then I had to step up into the raised vehicle, which was some sort of older Bronco or Blazer I'd assumed based on its seating level and capacity. In my weakened condition, I could hardly hoist myself up, so they figured they'd help me out a little with a shove here and a push there. I finally found the seat and plopped into it unceremoniously. I wouldn't say it was the most comfortable ride I'd ever experienced, but it sure beat the hell out of the seat I'd occupied for the last week.

After turning my head, I soon realized that the tape was coming loose. I could see out of the corner of my eye, and it was cloudy and raining. One of my captors held a gun, but it was down below the window line so, to fellow passers-by, we appeared to be just a few guys heading for a local nightspot to down a beer or two. Next to me was one of my male captors, and in the front seat sat the driver and a woman I'd never seen before. I didn't recognize any of them, and somehow this surprised me.

I sat perfectly still, used to that by this time, waiting to see what they were going to do with me. The ride was rough, and every bump and jog in the road made my body cry out and my patches slip down that much further. I tried to see if there were automatic locks on the door in case I needed to make a quick get-away. I worried that if I bailed, they'd just turn back around and run over my ass. Or, it would be my luck, I'd escape to an empty parking lot when their plans were to take me to my family and make the exchange. Then they'd have to shoot me just before I was about to go home.

I took inventory of my new set of chains. Smaller ones had been used so as not to be conspicuous in public. They wrapped them around each wrist like handcuffs. The chains were locked in the front instead of the back, and the same was done to my feet. If I only knew whether I was being taken to my family or my death, then I'd know what to do! Business had taught me to think on my feet, so I'd just have to depend on that when the time came and hope my head was clear, my body ready for flight, and my will to live stronger than their will to kill.

Suddenly, my thoughts were interrupted by the vehicle as it came to an abrupt stop. Again, I heard one door open and then slam, but this time there were no others that followed. Soon the windows went down, and I could smell diesel engines. We were at a truck stop somewhere, and I could make out the distinctive front end of a semi truck. Even though the car was very loud, I could hear my captor calling on the phone. He jabbered something in his native tongue, and then the phone was thrust through the window. I acted like I couldn't see the phone, so he whacked me with it to get my attention. "*Señor, teléfono.*"

"Hello," I croaked, amazed at the hoarseness of my own voice.

Chapter Eleven:
Would Today be the Day?

"Who am I speaking to?" It was the voice of a young female. "Who was she," I wondered.

"This is Ken." The phone was quickly jerked out of my grasp.

"No police!" he shouted into the phone. Then he talked for another two to three minutes in Spanish. Oh, how I wished I spoke the language. "What the hell were they talking about?"

"*Señor*," he yelled, slamming the phone back into my hand.

"Hello?" I answered.

"Ken, what is the N (vehicle identification number) of your aircraft?"

My heart leapt. I knew someone from my family was involved in this call and that the woman on the other line was on my side. I gladly gave it to her, betting it was Keith that had come up with the question. He pulled the phone away again and said, "No police." They talked a few more minutes in Spanish, and then he slammed the phone down on the cradle. The window went back up. He walked around to his side of the car and got in. We sat there for a few minutes while they talked; I assumed their conversation was just more of the same that had gone on with the other person on the phone. I thought they were going to take me somewhere and release me, and my spirits were high with the anticipation of seeing my family again.

Another 30 minutes of driving, and then the car was parked for about five or ten minutes before anyone came to get me. The door beside me opened, and I felt instantly surrounded. I was going back into a house, but I didn't know where it was until they started disrobing me. Instantly, I recognized the smells and sounds of the prison where I'd been for so many days. They replaced the smaller chains with the heavier ones that had adorned me for almost two weeks now. Then, back my ass went into that damn wooden chair.

Now the voices, if at all possible, were raised higher than twice their usual volume. The leader of the group was pissed and making it clear to all those around him. Whatever had happened at that phone booth, didn't go as he expected. Gently, I tried to make conversation with them. "Problem?"

"No money . . . problem. Maybe *mañana.*"

"Dallas, family, doctor?" I asked.

"No doctor, no family." I could tell by the way they talked to me and the way I was being roughed up, that things had not gone well. Going to the bathroom or taking another shower was certainly out of the question, now. I desperately longed for a drink; even a slimy banana would be preferable to the acid eating at the lining of my nervous stomach. I realized that I was back for the duration and chained to this chair until perhaps what would be the end of my life. My spirits sunk to the lowest depth yet, and I settled back into the routine of slowly losing feeling, constant irritation and itching, excruciating pain, hallucinations, and the mental despair that accompanied the emotional trauma.

*   *   *

Things weren't going much better for my family, either. They were quickly reaching their breaking point as well. Keith had gotten himself pretty much banished from the FBI trailer that day. His temper got the best of his common sense when one of the agents divulged information to the local police, which they had asked the family not to do. He was understandably furious and, just like us Krusensterna men, willing to let her fly! In reality, it was the stress of the days of having to be controlled when he felt like losing it and having to be the man of the family when he was only 21 that were taking their toll. The FBI should have realized this.

From that point on, though, when an important call was being made, Keith was asked to step outside. Maria's heart went out to him. She knew what he'd been through and what a trooper he had been. If only every family member of a kidnap victim had someone like Keith, it would make the FBI's job 100 times easier. Try as she might to console him, he was devastated by the banishment and unable now to deliver information to the family. Their action only served to place everybody in the family on pins and needles.

Thank God for the naivete of my family; if they had known the true statistics of kidnapped victims who had lived to return home to their families unharmed, they would have been this side of hysterical. Deanne was doing all she could to keep Corinne and Beth calm, but she was in need of some calming herself. Her fiancee, Gerald, had come up to keep her company and give her some much needed support as well, but it was difficult to distract her from the pain and hurt she was feeling.

Otillio was still in exile. He occasionally came into the office to check on things, but never at a time when he could be caught alone. His children weren't going to school, and his wife wasn't going to work. They were hiding out, but he couldn't keep this up for much longer. There was a company to manage, invoices to log and pay and workers that depended on him. He knew if I was still alive, I would be counting on him to keep things going with the business.

Otillio did his best to stay free, alive and in control. He kept in close contact with Ron Coronado. Blanca, my secretary at the Reynosa office, did her best to maintain an air of normalcy around the place. I'm sure it was tough for her, too. Fear ran high in both her and Otillio's minds as one day stretched to another and still no word!

I closed my eyes and dreamed. I fantasized about SWAT teams, at least three or four, bursting through the door to rescue me. I fantasized about picking up one of their fallen guns and leveling in on my captors. I fantasized about showering and shaving, wondering if I'd ever do either again. I slowly drifted off to sleep with those wonderful images dancing through my mind until the reality of morning came biting at the heals of the horrors another day would bring.

CHAPTER TWELVE
Mañana

"*M*añana . . . hey *gringo* . . . *mucho* money, mañana!"

That dirty "M" word—mañana—had become the most irritating word in the Spanish language. I had worked in Mexico long enough to realize that much of their culture is based around the philosophy of "Why do today what can be postponed until tomorrow?" However, deep down I knew that I might not have another day in me. I might not be able to survive one more beating or one more day without water or food. Even if my body could withstand this kind of torture, I began to question whether my mind would hold up. Each day, I was finding it more and more difficult to bring my thoughts under control, and that seemed to frighten me as much as the shouted threats of my captors.

"Hey *señor*—mañana—money!"

There it was again, the cruel Mexican taunts that barged through my floating thoughts, insistent on bringing me back to the horror of what had become my daily reality. Why were they so excited? Why were they shouting about money coming tomorrow? They had been holding a mañana celebration since last night, and mañana was finally here. Did this mean there was a chance I'd be home in Texas today? I didn't want to allow myself any false hope, but my mind, once again, refused to obey. Instead, it was convincing me that today would be the day I would see freedom, and with the hope came a spark of energy and a desire to fight for life again!

During the last few days, I had lost that spark! I focused on the real possibility of what it would be like to face death. What would my family go through? What would happen to all those workers in my company who depend on me to provide an income for them? There's one thing about hope, though—it has a way of cropping up at the most unlikely times, even in the throws of death.

Another drunken, hung-over voice spitting his foul breath in my face, saying, "*Gringo* . . . family . . . money!"

It was early in the morning, but their partying had gone on all night. "What?" I asked, not fully awake and unable to understand exactly what he was getting at.

"Today . . . mucho money!" He was jubilant, if one could call his slurred laughter spewing between his smelling lips that of jubilation.

"Home? Dallas?" I asked.

"Ssshhh! Boom!" He laughed once more, striking me on the side of the head with a sloppy fist that refused to respond to the blurred orders his mind was putting out. I was used to it by now; the beatings had become a punctuation mark at the end of their loud conversations. More drunken laughter—more slugs to the head! I felt the warmth of dawn even though I couldn't see the light, but the residue of last night's sprawl was overpowering in the promising heat of the day!

Chapter Twelve:
Mañana

Still hope loomed on the horizon of this new day. God only knows why or how, but I felt that my spirits were up a bit this morning. It certainly wasn't from any tequila, and thinking back on it now, I really couldn't tell you where the feelings originated, but I was grateful for them all the same. Perhaps it was because my body knew what my mind had not yet comprehended. Today was the day for great plans—the day we would move forward to achieve great things. I began to realize where the hope came from—from my tireless belief in life!

More than ever, I realized that no matter what, my family had hung in there to the bitter end, working diligently to accomplish an almost impossible rescue. I couldn't give up now and let everybody down who had worked so hard to bring me to safety. I just couldn't believe the great life I had had so far was to end in a dirty shack in Mexico surrounded by these low-lifes! My dad didn't raise a quitter! There was that spark, just a little spark, but was I strong enough to turn it into a flame—a beacon for my family to find me? What if I got myself all revved up again only to wake up again and again to this living hell? I had often heard that a man could be best measured not by how strong he was or how smart he was or even by how many times he fell! Not that those things don't help in a crunch, but the true measurement of a man is taken by how often he is able to stand back up to life's challenges and tap that inner reserve of strength that enables him to fight another day. So, what about me? Was I tapped out? Could I stand just one more day?

This new day also brought returning pain in my legs and arms. The quick jaunt yesterday had been just long enough to allow the blood to flow back through my extremities. One would think I'd have welcomed the feelings I was experiencing, but I hadn't counted on the severity of the pain. It took my breath—like the tongue of a dragon, it burned and singed every muscle, every nerve end, every hair follicle. Like water to cracked earth, my body soaked up the newness of circulating blood and demanded more. The pain of it overwhelmed the pleasure of it, and I found myself close to passing out on more than one occasion during my short taste of freedom.

Now my body was complaining at the new binds that held me to the recliner, so I had to go back through the process all over again. First the heaviness of beginning numbness, then the stimulation to every nerve fiber—the march of thousands of tiny ants on their way to war with my body. After the stinging sensation passed, then my arms and legs would begin to cramp into knots of pain that kept me screaming on the inside. Fear of further beatings kept the screams down to whimpering moans. The more severe the pain, the more I'd sweat, and the sweating attracted real pests of every kind. Sometimes it was difficult for me to distinguish the real stinging insects from those feeding off my imagination and nerves.

Finally, after the pain had died down to endless numbness again, I'd begin to relax for a few minutes. Just a few, though, before the itching would begin. My nose itched, my beard itched, and every crevice and wrinkle in my body itched—but no relief! As the sweat pooled inside the bends of my arms, welts formed. The backs of my knees, my neck and the bends of my arms bled as if I'd been cut by a sharpened blade. I've heard it said that people can bleed through the pores of their skin under extreme stress. The kind of stress that kills! Perhaps that's what was happening to me.

Although yesterday's shower had been refreshing, now I suffered from the dampness it had left tightly tucked inside every fold, every indention of skin. I guess my captors felt the shower was luxury enough for me, so no fluffy towels were provided. Hell, I would have settled for an old bed sheet as long as it soaked up the dampness. Not knowing what the dampness would create, I had enjoyed the excess water, reveling in its feel on my dry, scaly skin. Now I was paying for just that slightest of pleasures. What had been tepid water running over my body, now felt like lava burning its way to the bone! Life could hardly get much worse. I didn't know what treats the guys had in store for me today, but I did know I was just about ready to give it up.

Oh, there went the signal, again. A tap on the window; a knock on the door! What usually followed was some quick conversation and then more television. If it was an especially active day, I'd hear the moans and grunts of "Sex Man," having his afternoon delight. For the life of me, I couldn't see how anyone could be physically stimulated by the smells and sights in that room. To this day it escapes me what was so sexy about a chained, naked, dying man that "Sex Man" couldn't keep his hands off the lady. I was just thankful he had an eye for the ladies and preferred that variety, if you know what I mean.

Every once in a while my mind amazed me at the ducks and turns and empty avenues it took through my rambling thoughts. I wasn't allowed, not this morning at least,

Terror In Mexico:
The Kidnapping of Ken Krusensterna

to spend much time alone with my thoughts. When I finally focused, I sensed several people hovering around me, which was something that didn't happen first thing in the morning. I became very still—waiting for what was to come. Another beating? Would they shoot me? Stillness. Quiet. Waiting.

I flinched as one touched me, fearing a stab in my side or the barrel of a gun put in my mouth. Instead, what I felt was them fumbling with my blindfolds. Oooohhh, this didn't look good. I knew they would not want me to see them if they planned to keep their word and trade me for the money. The blindfold fell, but I squinted my eyes shut not wanting this to be the last thing I should see before they killed me. I was terrified, panic stricken, determined to die immediately and cheat them out of watching me squirm.

For the first time, I calmed when I heard that familiar voice say, "No look . . . boom!" I never thought I'd hear myself admit my relief at being threatened by my kidnapper, but I knew if they were still only threatening, I was relatively safe. Should I dare a peek? "Okay, open them Ken—open them and let's see what happens next." Although I commanded my eyes to open, they had a plan all their own, and it didn't include letting in that blinding light after having been deprived of sight for almost two weeks.

Actually, eyes are quite sensitive, and it doesn't take long for them to form their own defenses, which is what mine did. Over the past two weeks, my lids had nestled themselves into the crusty matting of liquid that sealed them from the horrors the rest of my body was forced to face. They could shut out intruding objects or over-zealous kidnappers, whatever the case may be. I'm sure I could have talked them into opening in a while, but my captors had no patience for my weakened condition. One jerked my chin front and center while another pried my eyes open, ripping my lashes and causing a constant flow of tears down my dirty cheeks.

It's funny what one will think in desperate times, and I guess I'm really no different. There I was, helplessly tearing, and all I could think about was the precious liquid I was losing through those tears. I hadn't been able to urinate in almost 24 hours, and it was scaring me more than the beatings I'd receive each time I wet on myself and subjected them to smelling me for the rest of the afternoon. It had even become like a game to me to see if I could urinate first thing in the morning, so they'd have to smell it during the heat of the afternoon. But, that game had no winners because I wasn't going anywhere either, and I had to sit in the stuff!

My vision was swimming, but after a while it cleared to a mild float, and the shapes around began to come into focus. I tried to stare straight ahead and refused to look at anyone in particular. I couldn't help but see them though, and I feared I had signed my death certificate. There they were, dressed in their look-alike Ninja outfits.

"Look!" one demanded, taking both his hands and directing my head to his designated target.

I squished my eyes together to try and make out the unidentifiable mound squatting down in front of my chair.

"Look!" he said again.

"What?" I asked. Truly, I couldn't make out what I was supposed to be looking at.

"Rosa's mama!" I concentrated hard to make out the person sitting across from me.

Terror In Mexico:
The Kidnapping of Ken Krusensterna

"Hi," she said weakly, in a pitiful attempt to appear as desperate as I was. I just sat there for a minute more confused and nearly blind. What was the meaning of this? What did they want from me, now? She slowly came into focus, and I could make out her clothing as my eyes moved across her body and up to her face.

"What the hell is this?" I whispered. I wondered if they expected me to be falling for more of their shit, whatever it was they were trying to pull. There sat Rosa's mama, supposedly held captive the same as me. She wore this Disneyland sweatshirt that was once upon a time purplish in color. Her arms were behind her, but even in my vision-impaired state, I could see that they weren't tied. Her feet were obviously not bound either. There was no nude, recliner experience for Rosa's mom—no siree! Not that I would wish that on anybody, but if she was being held captive, she was being held in "Hollywood" conditions, while I was tied in a shack in the jungles of Vietnam!

The clincher was her hair. Mama's hairdresser had definitely prepared her hair for the occasion. Very fat hair—teased out to add a few inches to her small stature. This morning, Mama looked as though she had just stepped out of her beauty parlor. Perfect makeup, perfect hair (if you go for that balloon type style), and perfectly tidy and clean clothes, even though they were mismatched and about three sizes too small. She was the vision of loveliness, another ray of sunshine to add to my already tormented sight.

I couldn't put my finger on it, but there was something about that hair that nagged at me. They had a blindfold on her as well, but something was strange about it. That's it! Mine felt like a vice grip wrapped around my head, and I worried I'd come out of this thing looking like Mr. Peanut, but Mama's was altogether different. There was no dent, no bulging, no reddened skin around the blindfold, nothing that would mess her do! Mama had made sure that the blindfold was gracefully draped around her freshly coifed style like a halo would sit on the head of an angel. The blindfold had been purposefully placed around her eyes like a tiara on a beauty queen.

"Ugh . . ." I grunted, not wanting to let them see how alert and observant I really was. I didn't know what to say without giving away what I knew. I knew what I wanted to say—or rather YELL! "You BITCH! You and your daughter are conniving BITCHES! I hope you rot in hell and the worms eat you slowly!" That's what I really wanted to say, but I figured that would have drawn a few frowns from the crowd, not to mention it would have most likely gotten me killed. So, instead, I just let my head drop forward as if I was out, and they gave up their efforts.

Just as quickly as they had surrounded me to take the blindfolds off, they were around me again—putting them back on. Then it hit me. They must be planning on letting me go. Why else would they go through the trouble of showing me Rosa's mother? They were still trying to protect the two women. Did they think I would continue business as usual down here? Were they crazy? Well, that was the key, wasn't it—they were crazy, and I didn't want to do or say anything that would hurt my chances to get out of this alive.

I have always liked to consider myself a gentleman, but what I wanted to do to Rosa and her mama right that moment was unthinkable. I wanted to make it slow and

Terror In Mexico:
The Kidnapping of Ken Krusensterna

painful! I wanted them to come as close to death as I had. I wanted their lips to crack from the lack of fluid. I hate to admit it, but I wanted them to bleed. I needed to get away from these thoughts; hatred was eating my insides like the bugs were eating my outsides.

I allowed myself to think back on yesterday's activities. I wondered what the reaction of the girls and Keith had been when the woman on the phone had revealed the fact that I was alive? Had they cried and hugged each other? Of course they would be happy, but would they, like me, refuse to let hope overrule good judgment, choosing instead to discipline their minds and continue to wait for the outcome? Knowing what they could do to one's emotions, I wanted them to avoid harboring false hopes.

If they had gathered the money, how had they managed to do so? I was the only person with real access to any money in the family. Had someone helped them? I wondered if the police were involved back in Texas or maybe even the FBI! Now my mind was preoccupied with thoughts of my rescue instead of my death or the death of those involved in my torture. This was a much more productive, sane place for me to be, so I decided to give my rescue some focused attention. During my career, I had often been to motivational seminars and heard them say many times that what you give your thoughts to becomes your reality. If that was the case, I was thinking RESCUE all the way! Who would RESCUE me? When would I be RESCUED? What would the authorities do to my captors after my RESCUE? I faded in and out of consciousness that afternoon with the word "rescue" on my lips and in my thoughts.

CHAPTER THIRTEEN
The Shootout

I didn't know it at the time, but it wasn't just the FBI involved in my rescue attempts. This case went all the way up to Janet Reno's office. As I said earlier, politics were right for me at the time, and the FBI and my family had the full cooperation of the Mexican government. With the approval of the President of the United States, Reno had actually given the okay for a spy plane to search for me. Everything was a "GO" as soon as they had an answer as to the location where I was being held. With infrared lasers, they knew it was just a matter of time—but time was running out, and the weather was working against us.

With a successful trap and trace on the call, they now knew where the phone was. It had come from a phone in the plaza along Zaragosa Street in Reynosa. It was time to notify the Mexican officials with the information, as the FBI had no jurisdiction in Mexico. Of course, if push came to shove, it wouldn't be the first time the FBI had gone where they had no jurisdiction—I'm sure. One would think, in order to kidnap and hold ransom a corporate executive for almost two weeks, the *desperados* would need to have a complex plan. Not so! Their's was more the shoot-first-and-ask-questions-later philosophy. In fact, a plan may have given the FBI something to go on, but my kidnappers' erratic behavior and unpredictable methods offered no patterns, no clues and precious little time to try to hook on to something concrete. The FBI's only hope was Rosa, and if I got to the bitch first, they'd have nothing to go on.

In this case, the FBI's mainstay had to be the cooperation of the Mexican government. The law enforcement group in Mexico was very similar to our FBI, and it wasn't long after the trace had been confirmed that the kidnapper was identified. Alfredo Torres Zumaya! Yep—it was old Al, all right! Al had been spotted making another call to my family. Al was the ringleader caught with his pants down by the Tamaulipas State Police, the PGJ, and every other initialed official in Mexico. I hadn't paid much attention before, but it occurred to me while telling my story how many countries investigative arms to the government come complete with their own set of identifying initials. It's like they want to hide their name as well as their identity.

Well, Al wasn't going to be able to hide much longer. In fact, Al's afternoon was about to become rather unpleasant, and, although I didn't know it, I was about to have a front-row seat and it wouldn't be in that recliner.

Keith was beside himself. He felt like a caged lion, pacing back and forth, waiting for any morsel of news they might throw his way. He knew he had lost control, but God— what did they expect from him? This was his father! Even though stepping one foot inside the trailer was off limits for Keith, he was smart enough to pick up on the increased level of activity going on inside. Something was afoot. There were more "blackfeet" inside that trailer than an Indian uprising in the mid-west, and Keith wasn't about to be left out of the action for long. Just about the time he had made up his mind to enter at his own risk, finally, one of the agents came out and told him the good news: "We caught one of the kidnappers."

Keith was elated. "What now?" he asked, trying to stay clam after remembering what happened last time he let his emotions get the better of him.

"We send up the spy plane to see what we can find. It shouldn't be long now, Keith. We know your father is alive, and we know where one of his kidnappers is; it won't be long before the rat leads us to the pack. Hang in there—we'll bring your father home!"

It wasn't to be that easy, though. There were too many clouds for the plane to get off the ground. It seemed to me that it rained from the time I'd been grabbed. It was apparently going to continue to exhaust the FBI efforts to play hero to the cause. Let's face it, the FBI isn't going to get involved if they can't play heroes, are they? Not that they weren't great, and not that they didn't get the job done. But sometimes they got impressed with their own power and forgot that they were dealing with the lives of a father and his wife and kids and that they needed to know what was going on to feel any sort of comfort in a nightmarish situation.

Keith wanted a play-by-play from the Mexican authorities. Sure that would happen—when pigs fly! For a little while longer, Keith just had to sit tight; something no Krusensterna knows how to do well. The day passed in relative uneasiness. Finally, the skies overhead had cleared enough that they could send the plane up. In a matter of

Terror In Mexico:
The Kidnapping of Ken Krusensterna

minutes, it was flying over Reynosa in search of my prison. Kind of makes you wonder how many satellite dishes, spy planes, or whatever else the government has overhead are able to watch you inside your home tonight or inside your office building—inside the very fabric that makes your fingerprints on life unique? I guess I would be worried more, but it is the FBI's ability to go "where no spy plane had gone before" that gives me comfort in knowing how small our world is and how much of our lives are traced and recorded. I don't much believe in secrets anymore.

Back in Dallas, Deanne was starting to crack. She had to have just a few minutes away, so after more than a week at her mother's, she went home. She promised Corinne that she would be back in the morning. Poor Deanne had been carrying the weight of the world on her shoulders, and a few hours away would be just what the doctor ordered. She went back home to shower in her own bathroom and get some clean clothes. She was not willing to give up and resign herself to fears that she'd never see her father alive again; she just had to get away for a little time to recover herself. Before she left, though, Deanne left Beth with strict instructions and Corinne with orders to stay in bed.

It hurts me to think how much this terror had become a daily routine at the Krusensterna house. Can you imagine it being a reality to awaken each morning to a handful of suited strange men in your home? Can you imagine going through the tedious task of coordinating telephone pick-ups each time your phone rang during the day or night? Can you further imagine seeing others carry on their lives as if everything was normal, while longing for yours to return to that place?   If I were to survive this, I was determined to never take my "normal" existence for granted again.   I would wake every morning with thanks for my freedom, with appreciation for the simple things in life—like standing, breathing without a gag in my mouth, and being able to scratch a damn itch!

For me in Mexico, the rest of the day was passing in relative quietness.   I knew that it had to be the weekend because the children were playing outside for much of the day. Usually, they went to school and there would be a period of about six hours when there was no playful squeals outside to herald the innocence that could still manage to exist in this hardened town.   Today was different—they played their games outside while the bigger boys were playing their games inside. How I envied them their freedom. It seems that children, no matter what their nationality, speak the same language.   I enjoyed listening to them.   Soon, the joyful sounds died down, and so did the traffic. I knew another day was about gone, as I heard the familiar revving engines of the planes coming in; the last one of the night I guessed to be around 10:00 p.m. Maybe tomorrow I'll be rescued—maybe tomorrow! Little did I know that morning wouldn't find Ken Krusensterna stuck in the blessed recliner!   Never again would I have to sit there—or would I?

In the middle of the night, there came a knock at the door. Not the familiar signal, but a hard, relentless knock. Ever since I had been feeling these weird sensations of hope, I was alerted to anything out of the norm. What was this new knock? It wasn't one of my captors; they gave the signal. Could it be one of the neighbors? No—people weren't too

Terror In Mexico:
The Kidnapping of Ken Krusensterna

neighborly in this part of town; everybody fearfully minded their own business. Were they bringing women in to enjoy another night of celebration at my expense? I heard no laughter—no clinking of liquor bottles or rowdy shooting of the gun into the ceiling. So, what was this demanding knock?

Then BOOM! The door cracked open. There was glass flying everywhere and the sound of splintering wood filled my ears. Then the gunshots started. I could almost feel the heat from the bullets as they whizzed by my legs and arms, and once again I was under siege to survive. "Great," I thought. "I've withstood all this torture to be gunned down in a shootout!"

The shouting was piercing, and I could hear people running in every direction. Spanish was the official language of the shootout, so I was kept in the dark by more than just my blindfold. I listened eagerly for even one word I could recognize, but my mind kept coming up empty. Outside there were struggles going on with the belabored grunts and groans of men being beaten, slapped and perhaps even shot. "Jesus! Who could tell the good guys from the bad guys—certainly not me!"

I just kept thinking, "Shit—I'm going to die in this chair." Then I really started getting scared when my mind was jumping around as much as my cramped and stressed muscles. Could this be a rival kidnapping gang who heard about the money that was being collected? Were they going to steal me away? Was it the police—the FBI? Who the hell was here, anyway? It wasn't a lazy game of poker and a six pack of beer, that's for sure. These people meant business, they were playing to win and I was the prize ham!

160

Suddenly, I felt someone at my side. Gently, but quickly, the blindfolds came off. "Look," said a voice. I was reluctant to turn my head, and the stiffness in my neck made it almost impossible for me to do as the voice asked. The voice sounded friendly, but it could be the last cruel joke just before my death. There he was—Ninja man revisited. I began to recoil!

"No, no, not bad! This *policía*," he commented as he saw the fear in my eyes. I could see now that they all had on these black uniforms with patches that read PGJ, Policía, on them. They had on SWAT masks with infrared lights, and I was soon able to make out their faces. These were not the faces of unshaven, slovenly kidnappers. They were the clean-cut, compassionate faces of men who recognized suffering and wanted to help. That's all it took for me. I couldn't afford not to trust if trusting these men meant I could get out of this chair.

It wasn't long before they were fumbling with my locks, trying to get the chains off me, but they didn't have the key. I looked over to my left trying to show them where I thought the keys were, but my voice couldn't croak out even the simplest of one-syllable words. I looked sideways where officers were beating the shit out of "Sex Man." Yep, he would be the one having those keys—just keep on beating him—he was bound to hand them over sometime. Meanwhile, I just watched. There are some things I believe they do a whole lot better down in Mexico, especially when they're on your side. They interrogate so much more thoroughly than we do!

Among the Mexican Policía who were busily rounding up the offenders was an officer who spoke very good English.

Terror In Mexico:
The Kidnapping of Ken Krusensterna

He was the commandant's brother. "I think I heard it hit the floor," he said, referring to the key. They looked around, and, sure enough, there was the key, shinning up its promise of freedom. In no time at all, they had the chains off me, and I could finally breathe relief, if even for just a few short seconds.

"Yours?" one of the officers asked me, holding out my clothing.

"Yeah," I responded. I didn't really know how to put them back on. They were so cut up and blood soaked that they were hardly suitable for wearing. Not even a dousing of Downy could have gotten the stiffness out of these rags, but I wasn't going to sit around here naked all night. I managed to put the clothes back on, but the smell of them gagged me. They stunk to high heaven, and believe me, it was no pleasant aroma. I didn't care; I was free. I was covered! I was out of there!

The men seemed to be rounding up people from different rooms, at least one or two others. I wondered where Rosa was. I stared as Johnny Pedroza, my watchman, as he made an escape out the door. He wouldn't get far, I was sure. There were more police there than I've ever seen in one place. The Commandant's brother was very kind to me, and in his excellent English, he let me know that he was quite aware of my discomfort. I stood up and almost immediately had to sit back down, though I sat elsewhere. Every time I tried to stand, I would get extremely nauseous. I knew it was a combination of several things; exhaustion, nerves, dehydration—and perhaps a lot of relief!

"*Señor*, do you need to get some air?" he said to me.

"Yes, please." I whispered. He let me lean on him as we walked outside, and the way I smelled, that was a real sacrifice. I soon realized that I was still barefoot and the rough Mexican terrain, with all its stickers, was murder on my feet. "My shoes, please," I asked.

"Here," said someone, handing me a pair of ratty ass slippers. My expensive loafers, I'm sure, were long gone by now, probably dancing the night away at a club in downtown Reynosa. I didn't care; I would never look at these items of clothing again as long as I lived. I just didn't want to put my feet where those animals had put theirs. I didn't have a choice with this one, so I stuck my feet in the slippers and stepped outside in the night air. Painfully, I bent down as I got through the door, heaving my guts out. I vomited for what seemed like an eternity.

What I was throwing up, I'll never know. I had flat nothing in my stomach but perhaps a bug I'd swallowed by accident a time or two that was plastered to the lining. I had just gotten things under control for a brief minute, when one of the officers came outside with a Pepsi. There was a fridge in the house, and he had retrieved one for me. I almost gulped the whole thing down at once, although it hurt like hell as it burned a path down my throat. The sweet fluid proved to be too much for my sensitive stomach, and in no time at all, I was heaving that up as well.

I collapsed against one of the Suburbans the officers had parked outside the house. Then I noticed a gun lying on the ground, just a few feet away from me. At that same instant, I looked up to see one of my captors standing beside another car, handcuffed. I looked again at the gun and then

Terror In Mexico:
The Kidnapping of Ken Krusensterna

at him. It was oh so tempting. The Commandant's brother saw me looking at the two and came over to me. "*Señor*, you would like to have a word with the man?"

"Yeah, I would." I looked again at the gun.

"Oh, no *señor*, you are not a bad guy. He's a bad guy. You don't want to be in trouble, too." The hell I cared! I could easily have shot him dead. Then, I remembered the stories of Mexican prisons and knew that I could never spend another day imprisoned. My knees grew weak again, and I vomited that last spoonful of Pepsi. Someone brought me a plastic lawn chair from the porch where the captors had sat so many nights conversing with neighbors as if nothing unusual were going on.

"Breathe, *señor*." It was my friend again, trying to help me calm my stomach. I put my head between my hands and just rocked. I was trying not to get sick again, and just when the world stopped spinning, the Commandant was telling me, "Come on, *señor*. Come on." I looked up. There were at least 30 people there, as well as a photographer. This was the stuff movies were made of!

"Come in, *señor*," he prompted me again. Shaking, I followed, with the help of a couple of officers supporting my sides. I almost froze. They were leading me back into the house I had no desire to ever step foot in again. To smell the smells from this place or feel its evil was more than I could bear. Yet, they were pushing me toward the room, right up to the chair I had resided in for a lifetime, it seemed. I panicked! What was going on here? Were they going to cash in on the ransom? Was this some horrible trick? With so much corruption and poverty in Mexico, anything was possible. I closed my eyes and prayed that I had passed out and was dreaming this horrible rerun. Why in the hell would they be trying to put me back in that chair?

CHAPTER FOURTEEN
The Chase

The look of sheer terror in my eyes had to have alerted the man at my side. In an instant, a thousand thoughts went through my mind. Were these new Ninja men going to kidnap me for the ransom? Did the police have the idea that they might just cash in on the ransom demand? Was this just some sick joke and they were not really cops? What the hell was going on? "Noooooo!" I screamed. I began to fight the man with all my might as he took me by the arm back into that dreaded room. My booming voice sounded about as threatening as a wet kitten, and I could feel my body shutting down—but I was never going back into that chair again! NEVER!

Never say never! That's exactly where I was going, and no amount of protests on my part would stop them. "Okay, this is it! Just give it up, Ken! Die for God sakes! Die! You really don't want to be tortured anymore, and your family will get over it in time—just die!" I knew what it felt like for a death row inmate making his last walk to the "chair!" This would be my last walk; I was convinced of it! My dignity had left me, and I began to plead with them to just kill me. I couldn't go back to that chair! Please, just kill me and get it over with. I had no fluid left for tears, but I'm sure I'd have been crying if I could have. In fact, I had nothing left—nothing but despair!

"Oh no! *Señor*! It is for the prosecutor!" said the man. When he realized the fear he had drudged up, his administrations became a lot less persistent. He couldn't even begin to understand what was going on in my head. I was actually contemplating suicide to prevent them from putting me back in that chair. What if I had grabbed his gun and just done myself in right before I'd been returned to my family? Wow, would that be Hollywood, or what? I let him urge me forward but stood with my legs rigid against the chair. I couldn't bend them back into that position. Now the protest came from my body as well as my mind.

I looked up into the eyes of the man bracing me up so as not to injure me as he lowered me back into the chair. For some reason, I trusted this man. He seemed to have genuine concern for me and to this day, I appreciate his attention. It wasn't that I wanted to be difficult, but it was absolutely inconceivable for me to think I would have to sit in this chair for one more second.

"Okay, okay," I said. He slowly explained to me that they needed to take the pictures for evidence to give to the prosecutor. The courts in Mexico run differently than they do here. There really isn't a court system. Everything is handled between the judges and attorneys in closed chambers. But they still needed evidence; they needed to convince a judge of the horrors I had been through. After days, I managed to scrounge up the energy and moisture to cry. As the tears silently slid down my blood-stained face and the ravages showed against my pasty, white body, I was sure the judge would have no recourse but to throw the book at these men—and women, for that matter. Who couldn't see the horrors of what had gone on in that room? I had to giggle to myself, wondering how the judge would like to smell the room as well. Perhaps we could provide one of those "Scratch and Sniff" pictures and he could experience the whole enchilada.

Carefully, I was lowered down into the chair, and I began to shake, uncontrollably. I wasn't a hundred percent convinced that I wasn't going to be back there for another twelve days, and, obviously, neither was my mind. Then I went into shock! Not when they shot me in the head! Not when they stripped me, chained me to the chair and beat me repeatedly! Not when they robbed me of my dignity and threatened me with death! Nope, I decided to go into shock when I was told I was free—but I still had to sit down in that chair. I couldn't do that. My legs hardly wanted to move – it was as if they knew where they were going. I finally made it. I sat down and it felt different. For the first time, I understood how people could get used to the horrors of imprisonment, to feel almost at home in hell.

They didn't ask me to remove my clothes. They just laid the chains losely back over me. While my mind reacted, so did my body. As soon as I adopted the reclining position, my legs and arms began to assume their numbed state. About the time they were calling in the troops of stinging ants, the flash of the cameras further tortured my eyes, and it took everything I could do to keep it together. After what seemed like an eternity, they finished.

Chapter Fourteen:
The Chase

He asked if I wanted to go outside, but I was climbing out the chair before he could extend a helping hand. "Yes, yes," I said. As I went through the door again, I breathed in the outside air. For once, Reynosa didn't smell dirty—anything would have been better than the inside of that house.

I looked up to see the area swarming now with people. *Federales* were all over the place. There were more Suburbans than a Chevy dealership in a spring sale, and people in uniform were going everywhere dragging yellow caution tape behind them like ribbon candy. Then they came out with Rosa's mother. They walked her past me; her head was down and she was handcuffed. As much as I wanted to reach out and grab a handful of that hair, I only manage a soft, "why?" before she walked away. This time she'd be imprisoned for real. Why? What would make a usually sane woman, a mother, do such a thing? The answer came to mind before the words finished forming themselves. MONEY! MONEY! Lots of MONEY! Mama said nothing, just hung her head in shame and kept walking with the officials to an awaiting, black Suburban. I'm afraid I felt no pity and very little compassion for her at that time, and if truth be known I don't today. Whenever I think of Mama—I think of a cold-hearted, bitch determined to get her due.

Now the shock had set in, and I found myself wandering around when the ambulance pulled up. "*Hola, señor*," the paramedics said to me.

"Yes?" I answered skeptically. Spanish was not my language of choice right now.

"To the hospital, *vamanos*," they said.

"No, not here," I said stubbornly. I wasn't about to give

my captors another shot at me. "You're taking me to the United States. I won't go to the hospital here." Half dead and still a stubborn Krusensterna.

"*Sí, señor*, you need a doctor. You need hospital."

"I'd rather die in the United States than spend one more night in this country, do you understand?"

"Okay, okay, *señor*. We just take your vital statistics." They finally convinced me that they would just do it right there and that they wouldn't drag me to the hospital. I let them check my vitals, my blood pressure and anything else they could manage to reach, but I wasn't stepping one foot into that ambulance. For all I knew, they would drive me to another shack and chain me to another recliner. I saw very little of what was going on around me that night, except the ground as it neared my face and faded away each time I felt faint. However, one thing I did see was the paramedics taking my vital signs shaking their heads and whispering what they should do with me. I was determined to make a run for it if I saw any of them come near me with a needle. Yeah, who was I kidding? Make a run for it? I couldn't even walk—much less, run.

All this time they were trying to get me to hold water in my stomach. There was absolutely no way that I could. Everything that went into my mouth came right back out. After about 20 to 30 minutes of this, they gave up. All the time that these guys were working on me, the photographers had continued to snap pictures. I'm sure they got some great shots of stomach bile and caked blood. Vultures! There were vultures disguised as reporters and photographers wherever I looked, so the safest place for me to look was down.

At first I had to sit down or fall down, but I was feeling just a little better now. I got out of the ambulance I had so reluctantly sat in and found my one friend. He told me they were still going through the house and through evidence. He offered me the front seat of one of the Suburbans. Nice, shinny, new vehicles. I hated to think the smell I'd leave behind. The Suburban would probably have to be sprayed and dipped after this stray was dropped off. I wasted no time crawling up into the cool, comfortable seat, and for the first time in weeks I felt safe. A kind, young officer came up to me with a small bottle. "*Agua, señor?*" he asked.

"Thanks," I said. I knew the word was "*gracias;*" I just refused to say it. I slowly drank the water, hoping that finally some would stay down. No such luck! I saw the family next door come out. It was a man, his wife and his little kids, and I was better entertainment than late night television. So those were the voices I had heard outside for weeks. The voices now had faces.

"How did you find me?" I asked.

"Airplane," he said. I would later find out about the surveillance plane they had sent to check out the house before the raid. The plane and its tireless pilots had been up for 16 hours. Then I found out a bit of information that hit me in the gut. They had rescued me around 11:30 p.m. The guard had instructions to shoot me in the head if they weren't back by midnight. I was reeling from that bit of information when all of a sudden all hell broke loose again on the radios. There was a lot of chatter going on with the officials. All the police bands seemed to be going at once. "Get in the truck!" shouted one of the officers.

Terror In Mexico:
The Kidnapping of Ken Krusensterna

I was already in, but I buckled up. "Okay, I said. Where are we going?"

"We're going to get the bad guys."

Jesus—what the hell—going to get the bad guys? As much as I wanted to get them, right now all I wanted was a soft bed, a huge steak, a tank of water and my family. This was no time for a road chase. Now, I was wondering if I would survive the ride, and I could feel my insides churning again. "I've got to hold my head out the window," I said. They didn't seem to mind, and the chase was on—big, black Suburbans with a bunch of big brown men and one white head hanging out the front as if riding shotgun.

Our caravan went down a series of rutted streets with no lights and no sirens. My God, we were running people off the road, chancing their lives in order to catch the bad guys. How many more people would have to suffer before this would end? Traveling at about 80 mph, it was liable to end sooner than they anticipated.

We were flying, hitting pot holes and flinging so much mud up on the windshield that the wipers wouldn't work; they couldn't cut through the mud. I was getting sicker by the minute. I wanted to curl up and die; I was hurting from ass hole to appetite. All I could think was "Shit, I survived days of hell just to die in a police suburban." It seemed like hours but was probably no more than 30 minutes before we pulled up to a 7-Eleven. One of them asked me if I wanted anything to eat. My thoughts went back to childhood illnesses, and all I could think of was crackers. I didn't specify what kind and he came out with the type that have cheese on them. "No, no. Not that kind." I did my best to describe what I wanted, and finally he emerged with a small box of saltines and some water. I did my best to eat that.

I knew from the location of the 7-Eleven that we weren't far from Rosa's house. I had gotten out of the Suburban because I had to throw up. As I walked around, I noticed Rosa's mother in the front of one of the vehicles in between two *Federales*. I wanted to talk to her so badly; maybe I just wanted to beat her. I couldn't decide which. For an hour we waited there. "Why aren't you taking me to the U.S.?" I asked.

"Bad guys," they would answer. No more time for idle conversation. Here came the rest of the entourage and everyone shouted, "Back in the truck! Get in the truck, *señor*!" One of them pointed to a Suburban and said, "Rosa." If I was understanding them correctly, they had caught Rosa at her house. They told me that she wouldn't come out of the house and refused to let them in. In order to get her to cooperate, they finally told her that her mother had been shot. See what I mean by Mexican tactics. I loved it! Rosa came slinking out and they arrested her. Nobody read her her rights. Nobody asked her if she wanted to make a phone call. It was just lie to her and get her the hell out of there. YES!

Zoom! We were off and running again. I was almost longing for the stillness of my old recliner…okay maybe not, but this was making me sicker and sicker. I knew that the next thing that came out of my mouth would have to be my stomach. What else was in there? What stories these young men would have to tell tomorrow. "You wouldn't believe this old man we had in the truck tonight. He smelled like road kill and he threw up his stomach." Great stories for the kids and Grandma.

Terror In Mexico:
The Kidnapping of Ken Krusensterna

The closer we got to Reynosa, the more I began to recognize the local restaurants and nightclubs. I knew where we were. I had counted six cars altogether, but there was some strategy tactics going on behind us. We finally stopped, and two cars pulled up while the other four hid. I had to get out and sit on the curb and hang my head between my legs to keep from passing out. I was trying hard to keep the water down and poured a lot of it over my head in hopes that it would revive me. More than anything, I didn't want to wake up in a Mexican hospital.

Another hour passed when my friend came out, shouting, "We got the bad guy." The last one had been partying the night away in a dance club. Can you imagine? Not a care in the world—just dancing the night away in a nightclub, dreaming about being a wealthy man as soon as they got the money and disposed of the body. Now, I started getting angry. If we could just stay still long enough for me to stop throwing up, I'd show them all a thing or two. But I was not to have that luxury. In minutes, I was loaded up once again and driven to headquarters.

At headquarters I was lead into a large room containing about twenty people. Agent Cisnosis walked up and introduced himself. "Hello Kenneth. I'm Agent Cisnosis, and I'm glad we got you."

"How's my family?" I asked.

"Keith's at the border waiting for you. He's doing just fine."

"How about the girls?"

"They're frightened, but they've held up beautifully. You have a great family." He introduced me to the other five agents, including Maria. "Can I interview you, Ken?"

Chapter Fourteen:
The Chase

"No," I answered. "I need to go to a hospital."

"They really want you to stay in a hospital here, Ken."

"No, if I'm going to die, it's going to be on American soil. Not this fucking place." Maria came up and talked to me for a minute, trying to convince me to stay. "I just want to get the hell out of here."

"Will you talk to them before you go back to Dallas?"

"Yeah. I'll do that."

"It's a definite that you weren't involved in this thing," she said. I wanted to say, "No shit!" but instead, I did the right thing—just threw up again. While I was in the bathroom, I could hear them saying "We've got to get him to a doctor." If I had to crawl or swim, I was going home for treatment.

When I emerged from the bathroom a few minutes later, they got a confirmation from me that I would talk to the Mexican authorities before I left McAllen. Then, like a happy crowd at a high school reunion, everyone posed for pictures. I didn't participate, not really feeling like it was a Kodak moment. As we were leaving, I saw one of my captors being led up to the interrogation room. He didn't look any happier than I did, and that cheered me up, considerably. I wished him misery! I wished him to rot in a Mexican prison. I wished him dead! I have never admitted that before, but I wished him dead.

They loaded me into another Suburban and off we went. The drive this time wasn't very long and they didn't feel the need to fly through the streets. As we pulled up to the bridge, I saw the waiting ambulance. Then, another snag. I had no identification, so the border patrol had to thoroughly investigate before letting me cross. I was thinking I could just go back to the house and get my wallet and the thousand dollars that had been in it; I'm sure everything would be there. Or, perhaps everything was taken to police headquarters. Yeah, that's the ticket. I'll just call the *policía* and have them bring my money and wallet down to the border for me.

Sarcasm was getting me nowhere, and I really wanted to get back on home turf, so I set aside my emotions. I postponed the need to cry, to rant, to scream at these idiots that "I HAD NO I.D. BECAUSE I HAD JUST BEEN KIDNAPPED, SHOT, TORTURED FOR 12 DAYS AND STARVED HALF TO DEATH. FORGIVE ME IF I LOST MY I.D." Instead, I stayed quiet and let the *policía* handle everything. Eventually we were cleared to go and I stepped onto U.S. soil. I wanted to cry. The paramedics had the stretcher all ready for me and another battle ensued. The bastards wanted to strap me down! I fought like a caged animal. The hell they were going to tie me down for anything. "Damnit! I've been strapped down for 12 days! No one is tying me down again!"

"Sir, it's for your own safety. It's like a seat belt."

"I don't care. You're not tying me down." The agents talked to them for a bit and finally they agreed to leave me unrestrained. They checked my vitals and had to put I.V.'s in me, immediately. It was hot in the ambulance and I was moaning for them to "just get me to the hospital."

They jumped in the front and we took off. Of course, I fell over on the drive and they had to give me oxygen. It was a small price to pay for freedom, though. On and on we drove, through the streets of McAllen. All I could think of was clean, white hospital beds and a shower. Oh, and a razor. I had to have a razor. And my family. I felt myself start to drift again and I let the blessed sleep take over. I slept for only minutes before we pulled up to the hospital. There stood Keith. When they wheeled me up to him, we embraced. All I could say was, "I'm sorry."

"There's nothing to be sorry about, Dad. I love you." Finally, I cried. I cried like a baby in the arms of my 21-year-old son!

CHAPTER FIFTEEN
Recovery

Wheeled on the gurney past one room then another, I fantasized about getting cleaned up and into a fresh smelling bed. They finally reached my room, and I was quickly transferred from the stretcher to a bed. Great—soon the shower will come. I couldn't wait. WATER! All the water I could hold in my mouth at one time. All the water I could play under. All the water necessary to wash away the memories of this nightmare. Somehow, I didn't believe all the water in the Gulf could accomplish that feat.

To my disappointment, instead of a shower and a shave I got a shot of compazine. I had no idea how close I was to dying of dehydration, but the doctors did. They had to give me something to keep me from throwing up and then try to get some life-giving fluids in me. I looked up at the doctors—then I looked at the clock. It was 5:00 a.m. Good Lord, I had been rescued just before midnight, and for five hours those idiots had hauled my ass around Reynosa chasing the "bad guys."

I couldn't think about that right now, or I'd be adding others to my list of those I wanted done away with. Back to that shower I'd been craving. It wasn't to happen for quite some time. I guess if I could have stood up long enough to get under the water, that would have played a major role in talking the docs into letting me under the spray. But, my legs weren't working so well these days. My left arm was having problems with the circulation of blood, and I couldn't seem to focus on my thoughts. In fact, I couldn't do much more than try to mumble a few words before falling off to sleep with what seemed like a hundred needles in my body. I had become a human pin cushion.

I would nod off to sleep wondering when they would quit pumping all that saline and sugar into me. Much later, I found out that it wasn't saline and sugar water they were giving me for nutritional purposes—it was blood. I had lost pints of the stuff, and most of the medics were surprised that I had survived the whole thing. My clothing testified to my ordeal, and I could barely stand to look at the ragged remnants piled in the corner. In a few days, I was longing for a shower and clean clothes, a shave and a major overhaul of my emotions. It seemed like I was on an emotional roller coaster and riding first car headed on the downhill slide. I was a mess!

As if in answer to my prayers, I looked up and there was Beth sporting an armful of clean clothes. I embraced her and felt we both had released the tension of the past few weeks in one another's arms. We held tight, not wanting to let go. Finally, my tough Beth wiped her eyes and said, "I brought you clean clothes, Daddy." Such a thoughtful thing to do. I would soon learn all that my family had done while I was being held captive. They had, too, gone through their own private hell, captive to their fears. But, right now I was looking at clean clothes, and my fantasies were coming true.

Terror In Mexico:
The Kidnapping of Ken Krusensterna

Beth took one look at me and knew what I wanted. She called in Keith, and we men managed to get me out of that hateful hospital gown and those ratty-ass slippers that had followed me from the kidnapping scene. I threw on a green golf shirt, chino pants, and headed for the shower. I didn't know what was worse, my desire to eat or shower and shave, but by necessity the shower and shave came first. They agreed to the shower, but eating was definitely out of the question. Instead, I got the tiny, magic pill to help me sleep.

I slept like I'd never slept before. Hard sleep, lost in deep "no thought" dreams. I woke just briefly to see Keith and tell him to go get some sleep himself. Keith had done ten years worth of aging these last few weeks, and I believe he needed the sleep as much as I did. Finally, at about two that afternoon, both Beth and Keith were by my side. They were there as the doctor came in to examine me, and for the first time we had a chat.

It seemed I was visited by Mr. Death several times during that two week period. I related the story of seeing the bright lights and traveling down a dark tunnel and of feeling as though I had to make a choice of whether to come back to the pain or escape to this wonderful paradise forever. The doctor told me that was a common phenomenon for people who had experienced near death trauma. He told us that any one of the things that had happened to me was enough to kill—either the bullet to the head, the extreme blood loss, the dehydration or the emotional stress. Any way you looked at it, I could not have lived another day.

I couldn't seem to get enough of those showers, and when I came out of the shower that day I heard that Corinne and Deanne had called. They had been trying to reach me all night, but due to the high security around me, the hospital was denying that I was there. I completely understood why, but it was very frustrating for my two girls back home. Keith and Beth stayed with me that day and on through the next. We talked, we cried a little bit and I slept.

Here we are now—full circle into the story. If you'll remember, that's where my story began. That's when the poor aide made the mistake of bringing in a Mexican dish for my first meal. I must say, I felt much better now that Beth was there to battle the dragons for me. I heard the most amazing thing: Beth had offered to go take my place. For a moment I felt sorry for my kidnappers, and what would have happened to them if that had taken place. Beth would have cleared the house in less than an hour, strapped every one of the fuckers to a recliner and had them begging for mercy when the *policía* arrived.

I flew back to Dallas that Thursday, and my return home was almost more than I could take. There's nothing like being surrounded by the people you love. Not even the nightmares could dampen my enthusiasm for being home, but they came all the same. I believe my family was quite worried for me during this time, when each morning I'd awaken to the horrors of believing myself back in that dirty shack, chained naked to that evil recliner. To this day, I cannot even bear to kennel my dogs; the thought of putting them in a cage is beyond me.

Everybody went back to the normal lives we grow to expect and anticipate, but all was not normal with me. Perhaps it can never be after having experienced such trauma. When Beth went back to her ranch in Phoenix and her job as waitress at the Mexican restaurant, she was amazed at the reaction of her Mexican co-workers. They came to her and apologized for the behavior of their people, as if she somehow blamed them for the kidnapping. It brought Beth to a clearer understanding of the closeness of a people, so close that they feel responsible when one of their own does bad.

Then there was Keith, moving back to Wisconsin where he was sure not to see a lot of Hispanic people. For Keith, it is more than he can handle trying to be friendly to a people who remind him of a time in his life when he could have lost his dad. Keith will have to find his own comfort, his own way, and he usually does—in his own good time.

Of course, there is Deanne. Deanne went back to work and in one simple little file folder lying on her desk was hit with the impact of all that had gone on. It was to be her next assignment. Her first case coming back to work was to deal with a juvenile, 17-year-old, Hispanic who was guilty of aggravated kidnapping. Deanne quietly closed the folder, walked into her boss's office and calmly said, "I don't think it would be in the best interest of this child to have me as his case worker."

As for Corinne and I, well, our lives changed as well. You can't look at death in the eye without it having an effect on your life. I needed new scenery and a new lease on life. I just couldn't find peace in Dallas any more, so Corinne and I have moved to the open spaces of Arizona. I sold the business, and now I spend my days riding, writing, and preparing talks for corporations doing international business and needing to protect their employees from experiencing situations like mine.

I know what you're wondering—what happened to the kidnappers? Well, I'd love to tell you they all got life with no chance of parole, but that is so far from the truth that this story would read more like a fairytale if I tried to push that happily-ever-after ending off on you. Truth is; I don't really know what happened to them, but let me give you a little background on what I do know. I know that the four men involved had just been released from prison after having served five years on previous kidnapping charges.

My accountant tells me that statistics don't lie, so if I believe past statistics on how many people survive an ordeal similar to mine, I'd have to say their last kidnap victim didn't live to tell his or her story. For that, these brave kidnappers served only five years. Five years—that was their justice! If the ransom amount was equal to mine, $350,000, I'd say they made out like bandits—pardon the pun. With the economic times being what they are in Mexico, let me ask you, what did they have to lose? Five years of their lives to make that kind of money! And, chances are they can pay off some officials and never serve a day in prison. It makes working for a living a sucker's bet, don't you think?

What I'm trying to say is that whatever they got wasn't enough. It wasn't enough time in prison to pay for the heartbreak they put my family through. It wasn't enough punishment for all my pain and suffering and for all the physical and emotional leftovers I now have to deal with. It just wasn't enough—well, all but one that is. I did hear that one of the kidnappers was gunned down and killed in the resulting chase. As for the other three men, they are serving a jail term, but they don't have it too bad since Rosa's uncle represented them and is currently making sure they have everything they need to make life reasonably comfortable. Of course, that was in trade for them testifying to the fact that Rosa and her mama were victims in the kidnapping as well. You got it—the two women walked away, scott free. What incentive do they have to never do this sort of thing again? Absolutely none! Think about it—who will be their next victim?

If you have a corporation that does business in Mexico, it could be your sales manager or human resource person who is required to frequently travel across the border. Or, if your son or daughter like to party in Mexico, the next call you get could be a ransom demand. Let's say your spouse decides to take a shopping or fishing trip south of the border, it could be the love of your life that is kidnapped, shot and tortured. I don't know about you, but I'm ready to make sure these kidnappers' salaries are cut to zero. Here's my plan.

There was a purpose to this, and I'm on a mission to make sure that all who have died in similar circumstances before me didn't die in vain. My goal is to ensure that travelers into Mexico pull off their rose colored glasses or untie their blindfolds and enter into the country with full knowledge of the lurking dangers, the desperate people and desperate situations that lurk around every corner, and I do mean every corner. How do I envision carrying out my plan? Well, it hasn't been easy or inexpensive.

I had to take first things first. So, the very first thing I focused on after returning home was to regain my health and positive outlook on life. Not that some of the physical and emotional trauma still isn't lingering, but, for the most part, it's manageable. Next, I began to record and write down my experiences while these memories were fresh in my mind. That in itself has been a challenge—reliving a life-threatening situation wasn't something I eagerly anticipated. While writing the book, I've been researching the incidences of crime against foreigners in Mexico, and I can tell you it has been a painstaking, dirty job of which the statistics are staggering. If these statistics don't lie, we're all in jeopardy when traveling in Mexico.

How could this many people have been kidnapped, tortured, murdered, or just turn up missing—never to be found again. How could this happen and nothing be done about it to relieve the pain and suffering left behind? It became unfathomable to even consider that the figures in these statistical reports were accurate. That literally hundreds of people's lives had been so permanently altered, and nobody was the wiser. No government official, public figure, politician, religious leader or military big shot had chosen to champion this cause and protect people from the horrors of terrorism committed right under our noses by our neighboring countrymen.

I've been taught all my life to stand up for my principles and that one man with a just cause could make a difference. Well, if this is true, then this whole kidnapping thing happened to the wrong man. It was time for me to take a stand—to make a difference. It was those thoughts that brought about my new company called STAND INTERNATIONAL. It's through Stand International that my ordeal has meaning; it's through Stand International that I can make a difference! What is Stand International? Thought you'd never ask!

Stand International is a new "preventative medicine" for corporate security provided to their employees who travel to Mexico. I travel all over the country and speak to organizations about how to keep their people safe while traveling into Mexico. Not only do I tell my story, but I also give them new insight into the Mexican culture and practices and into their beliefs and philosophies. I help them to help themselves.

Sometimes the simplest of habits could help you, your loved one or one of your employees to avoid becoming one of those dreadful Mexican statistics. You don't necessarily need an armored car and private bodyguard to ensure your safety, but you do need to show precaution while in a foreign country, especially one as volatile as Mexico. In fact, my development team is currently gathering data and putting together an easy-to-follow manual of what and what not to do—what and what not to say—what and what not to expect—when traveling across that border.

If you already live in the southwestern part of the United States, Mexico's border towns may look quite similar to those on the U.S. side, but don't let their appearance fool you. The line separating the U.S. side from the Mexican side couldn't be more definite. Although we are on the same continent, we are worlds apart. If all the voices of the dead, all the voices of the victims could rise together, their warnings would be deafening. If all those prospering from foreign trade could imagine the long-lasting affect this would have on their businesses, I don't understand how they wouldn't be pressuring the government to take an active role in exacting retribution to the offenders. After all, not only are they holding Americans and other business and personal travelers up for ransom, but their own people suffer the hits on their reputations and good will that they've spent years trying to build.

So, what's to be done? First of all, we have to be informed, educated, taught to be ideal citizens while traveling in a foreign country. And, we need to be prepared for the unexpected to happen, prepared to do whatever it takes to stay safe. We must be aware of, and 100 percent responsible for, our actions. We, as Americans, must take advantage of great business opportunities without taking advantage of their people. As far fetched as it might seem, every time you "cut a great deal" at the expense of the Mexican people or at the sacrifice of your integrity, you may have to face much more than you bargained for in the process.

The next two chapters are going to give you a reality check! What do you need to know? What do you need to do with the information you have discovered? How can you use this information to affect change in your lives and the lives of those around you who just might be traveling to Mexico in the near future? It could be simple, like something I did just a few weeks ago. Some friends of mine were going on a thrill-of-a-lifetime vacation to Cancun. Without putting a damper on their plans, I was able to offer a few pointers that might protect them along the way. They ended up having a wonderful experience. Now, would they have had the same experience had they not taken heed of my warning—maybe

Terror In Mexico:
The Kidnapping of Ken Krusensterna

so—maybe not! Who's to say? What I can say is that they returned safe and sound, and I'm expecting them to pull out those dreaded, vacation slides on my next visit. I'll make you a deal—if you promise not to show me your vacation slides, I'll give you a few pointers in the last couple of chapters that will give you added confidence on your next visit to Mexico.

As you look at the statistics in these last chapters, keep in mind that not all people become a statistic. In fact, the majority of Mexico's visitors enjoy a wonderful experience and recommend it to all their friends. But, let me ask you— what if you're the latest member of that elite group that gets transported across the border in a pine box? What if it's your family that is victimized, your company that loses its personnel and products? What if all your challenges while traveling could have been avoided if you'd just taken the time to read the story of someone who has had a first-hand encounter of the dangerous kind?

The following people you'll read about are not only statistics, they're flesh and blood people—even though they were treated as contributing figures in the latest police report or corporate security analysis. They were people, just like you and me, with families who loved them and business associates who depended on them to help support their families. They were sons, daughters, fathers, mothers, CEOs, salespeople, and they could have been your best college buddies out for a weekend adventure on the beautiful beaches of Mexico. Were they behaving without thinking? Absolutely! Were they breaking the law? Could have been! Did they deserve to die? Read the next chapter, and you be the judge!

CHAPTER SIXTEEN
It Could Happen to You!

As Americans, we often take for granted our inalienable rights and freedoms. Because we live in the United States, we don't expect to have to worry when traveling from Arizona into Nevada that we'll be stopped by a jeep full of dark-suited, armed men and given the choice between paying them a king's ransom for protection or death. I have yet to see in this country an advisory warning or travel alert on television for travelers entering a high-crime zone. Not that the United States is crime-free, but we feel safe to travel without the fears of being put in prison on bogus charges or shot and tortured over the contents of our wallets.

These are standard procedures in Mexico's interior. Not only do foreigners enter at their own risk, ready to battle the onslaught of kidnappers, murderers and your run-of-the-mill pickpockets and burglars, but Mexico's own citizens must also be on the alert for criminal activities. From sleepy little villages to busy metropolises, you never know when the *desperados* will strike. It has become so prevalent, that should it take you a day to read through this book, three more kidnappings will have happened in Mexico. Kidnappings

Terror In Mexico:
The Kidnapping of Ken Krusensterna

average 1,000 per year . . . mine was just one story in which the victim was lucky enough to live to tell about it.

In order to properly prepare and protect yourself, you have to first believe the possibilities that what happened to me could just as easily have happened to you. Let me sharpen the picture and make your understanding a bit more complete by enlightening you with a few of the more well-known kidnappings in Mexico. While American abductions in Mexico are some of the most brutal and include lengthy negotiations resulting in starvation, sexual abuse, mutilation and murder, Americans are not the only people who fall victim to these kidnapping rings. With Mexico's major cities reporting a 100 percent increase in violent crimes over the past five years, nobody is exempt.

Corporate Casualties

The Kidnapping of a Chrysler Executive

In June of 1998, an executive for Chrysler was kidnapped and held in his kidnapper's shack for 25 days before ransom demands were made. Though his care included some luxury items like minute amounts of food and water, and the facilities offered all the comforts of home, minus "sex man" and daily beatings, his emotional trauma was quite similar to that which I experienced. He believed he would never see his home and family again and that he'd die a horrible death at the hands of his cruel tormentors. Can you imagine that every day for 25 days this Chrysler executive awoke to the same depression, the same helpless feelings of the doomed, and the same calculating yet ignorant kidnapper's thwarted wants and ongoing acts out frustrations as I did? Those are the times when 25 days can be an eternity!

Like other victims, he did nothing to deserve this negative attention. It wasn't as if he was a tyrant businessman who victimized the people until they exacted retribution. He was an honest man trying to make an honest living in Mexico, which is difficult to do these days. He wasn't the sort who went looking for trouble, but it came looking for him. During his kidnapping, eight armed men rushed Automotores de Mexico, S.A., which is one of Chrysler's main dealerships south of the border. After the successful, mid-day raid on the dealership, he was taken to a house and held for several days before any of his captors even attempted to contact his family with the ransom demands.

In the final days of his captivity, there was a "bigger-than-life" shootout where five suspects were arrested, one being Alberto Alba Alba, a former police officer. Trying to escape, Alberto was wounded and suffered a broken leg, but other than that, nobody knows what happened to the other kidnappers. As in my story, the victim received no closure or satisfaction other than escaping with his life. And since the majority of kidnappings result in the deaths of their victims, God knows he had reason to feel elation. How much did his family or his company have to pay? Unknown!

President of Sony—San Diego

Up to just a few months ago, most Sony executives felt perfectly safe doing business with our neighbors in Mexico. However, with the recent kidnapping in Mexico City of their

Terror In Mexico:
The Kidnapping of Ken Krusensterna

San Diego based president of Sony electronics, corporate executives are rethinking their mistaken views. One evening, after a company softball game, two men forced Mamoru Konno into a vehicle and drove away, according to eyewitnesses. The two gunmen had accosted Mamoru Konno as he walked to his car after the game. They hid him in a remote area dense with mesquite bushes and vegetable fields on the outskirts of town.

In order to ensure his own safety, Mamoru was forced to call Sony on behalf of the kidnappers and demand $2 million. For reasons of discretion, Sony decided to pay the ransom and keep the police out of the loop—probably a good call on their part, considering most fare poorly in these kidnapping situations and the bad publicity could have been devastating for the company. Konno was eventually released, but the details of his capture, ransom and release still remain a mystery.

The Residents Resist

Kidnapping Mexico's Own

Mexican citizens are smarter and more culturally aware than their foreign counterparts when it comes to handling a kidnapping. They recognize the dangers and know the deadly statistics involving these gangs of kidnappers, so cooperation is more extensive and privacy more protected. One such case was that of a high school student in an affluent Mexican neighborhood. As the police investigated the disappearance of one student, they soon discovered that nine others had recently disappeared in that same area under suspiciously similar circumstances. All 10 people, it seems, had been taken hostage and held for ransom. Like many kidnappings in Mexico, the families paid the ransom and kept it from the local police.

* * *

In another case, the family of a businessman living in Mexico City who asked not to be identified, shared some of their horrors. I quote from the Washington Post: "After one and half weeks we reached the first impasses, and they said, 'If you don't send cash, we're going to send you his right hand in a bag.'" Family members thought they were bluffing when they didn't received another call for two days. The businessman's routine had been broken, which is always cause to be worried. When they did receive a call, it went something like this: "Did you get the packet? We threw a packet over the fence with your brother's hand. Go look," they commented sarcastically before hanging up the phone. Needless to say, the mutilation worked, and family members succumbed to the psychological threats and promises of continued mutilation.

* * *

Hotel owner, Miguel Ocampo, was kidnapped by armed men at his hotel. A maid witnessing the attack told officials later that the men kept hitting Ocampo over the head with the butt of a rifle and dragged him bleeding from his office. Even with eye witnesses, Ocampo was never found and his assailants never brought to justice. Once again, families suffer the unimaginable loss of a loved one with no satisfaction.

* * *

Gerardo Rosendez was kidnapped and a $100,000 ransom was paid by his father, Francisco. Still the captors did not return his son, and Francisco paid the ransom again. His son was never brought home! All Francisco has to show for his torment and personal sacrifices are a lifetime of debt and the belief that his son will now never be returned alive.

* * *

The son of small business owner Oscar Diaz was contacted with a ransom demand for his father, which the son paid with the money received from the sale of his father's ten cows. Although Oscar Diaz, Jr., paid the ransom, he did not hear from his father or the kidnappers. Having observed circling vultures flying close to the property where it was thought his father had been captured, neighbors encouraged the son to check it out. Sure enough, upon investigating the cause of the scavengers, Oscar Diaz, Jr., finally located his father—many days too late. This kidnapping took place in the small town of El Tiqui, Guerrero, where 30 of the town's 2,000 residents have been kidnapped.

* * *

Even if your family is able and willing to pay the ransom for the safe return of their loved ones, this business comes with no guarantees. You are not dealing with men of their words. Businessman Melchor Perusquia's family discovered this the hard way when they paid $390,000 only to have his dead body returned for their efforts.

* * *

Vincent Carroza, a New Yorker who manages Acapulco's Princess Hotel was held for 8 days during the Christmas season before he was released. The terms of payment were undisclosed, and the dirty business was completed quickly and quietly!

Officials and Celebrities

The Kidnapping of Government Officials and Celebrities

Even high government officials are not protected from the rampant kidnappings in Mexico's major cities and smaller towns. The Mexican finance minister's granddaughter was kidnapped by a gang working out of Mexico City. Believing his best bet to get her out alive was to conduct the business privately, we know little of what happened to her or to her abductors.

* * *

In February of 1999, I read about the kidnapping of Alvaro Campos, the father of soccer star, Jorge Campos. Jorge was the pride and joy of Mexico, the country's goalkeeper in the 1994 and 1998 World Cup Tournaments.

Terror In Mexico:
The Kidnapping of Ken Krusensterna

He had been getting threats since December of the previous year, but had refused to take any of them seriously. Luckily, Campos was finally released—unharmed. Was ransom paid—couldn't say for sure!

* * *

A singer, Vincente Fernandez, knows what it's like to sweat blood and give your all to have your son safely returned. Not too long ago he paid $3.2 million. Even though his son was returned, it wasn't without incredible emotional and physical scars. During the ordeal, the kidnappers cut off two of the boy's fingers. The 14-year-old was held for four months before being released, so there's no telling what kind of emotional trauma he'll experience in the years to come.

The Assailants

Profiles of the Perpetrators
The only things more despicable than these random acts of violence are those who commit them. Daniel Arimendi Lopez, known as the "ear lopper" was finally arrested in August of 1998 after an extensive, nine-month manhunt to apprehend the notorious murderer and kidnapper. Lopez was awarded this lovely nickname because of the grizzly way he handled his kidnappings. He was renowned for lopping off the ears of his victims and sending them to the families as proof that he had them. His kidnapping strategies were not lost on the victims that could

not physically withstand his particular form of torture. To convince one dead victim's relatives that even though their loved one was earless he was still alive, he applied a generous amount of makeup in an attempt to make him look animated and worthy of paying the ransom.

At his hearing, Lopez casually admitted to 21 kidnappings in three years. Although the gruesome details of this kidnapper are unthinkable, what made his presence in these kidnapping gangs so chilling was that he was a former Morelos state police officer. His gang members were equally as creative and connected—five were police officers. At the ripe old age of 39, Lopez had managed to muster up a gang of nearly 40 kidnappers. His little helpers were necessary to sharpen the butcher's shears and hold the victims down while he cut off their ears without the comfort of even an aspirin to dull the pain. Lopez ceremoniously had his victims bound, pushed to the floor and then sliced. When the job wasn't done to his satisfaction, he resorted to killing his helpers. He sliced and raped his way almost through to the heart of one female victim, threatening to cut her breast off if ransom was not received within his unreasonable time frame. Although his three-year crime spree netted him close to $30 million, he claimed he ". . . never did it for the money." He just wanted to see if he could get away with it and that he was in it for the thrill of the kill!

* * *

The same month that I was kidnapped, a New York University graduate student, Frederick McPhail, died after a group of Mexico City Police Officers allegedly abducted him

Terror In Mexico:
The Kidnapping of Ken Krusensterna

and drove him to cash machines forcing him to withdraw money. They then made him drink large quantities of alcohol, hoping it would cloud his memory. Instead, it killed him. Thirteen police officers, all members of a kidnapping gang, have been arrested, but Frederick McPhail never lived to see his 28th birthday.

* * *

Kidnappers near the California border killed two men living in the United States when their families paid only a portion of the $1 million ransom they were demanding. The families could raise only $145,000. They desperately drove it down to Tijuana and left it, as instructed, in a car with its engine running. The kidnappers were angered with this small amount, killed the men and buried them under the floor of a local auto repair shop.

Methods of Kidnapping

Creative Kidnapping
Today's kidnappers are getting quite innovative. They have now devised extortion methods that are less risky and more cost efficient than the previously preferred long-term kidnappings. One of the latest trends is called "Kidnap Express." It's one of those no mess, little stress kidnappings since the victims are usually grabbed on the street, put in a car and released several hours later after having surrendered everything he or she could obtain within a short

period of time. It might be $1,000 in their wallet, their Rolex or the gold in their teeth—a real hands-on kidnapping technique!

Belgian businessman, Jean Pierre Liebers, was one such victim. His perpetrators grabbed him and forced him to withdraw large sums of money from his American bank account as well as his Mexican accounts. Once they had wiped him out, he was free to go.

Another type of new kidnapping is the "Virtual Kidnapping." This is an ingenious plan, really. A member of the gang—usually a handsome, well-spoken, expensively dressed Latino male—strikes up a conversation with a lone woman frequenting a bar in the evening. Once he has determined that she is not traveling with her family, the gentleman carries on a lengthy, very interesting and useable conversation with the woman. He'll be busy for an hour or more gathering intimate details from her, those she sees no problem in offering. It could be her pet's name, where she lives, what she does for a living—any type of useful information that will let the innocent family back home know that this captor speaks the serious truth.

Next, the criminal will convince the woman to go on one of the great tours offered by her hotel, making sure it will last for at least four or more hours. This gives him and his companions in crime enough time to contact her family to tell them she's been kidnapped. They convince them with believable evidence gathered during their conversation with the unsuspecting woman. By the time she returns from her wonderful tour, her family's bank account is wiped out and so is her dignity.

Terror In Mexico:
The Kidnapping of Ken Krusensterna

With all these kidnappings taking place one after another, seemingly right under the nose of the Mexican government, it seems logical to question why nothing is being done to put a stop to them. Why don't their law enforcement officers take care of these situations? After all, eventually, foreigners are going to stop spending their hard earned dollars traveling to Mexico and then trying to get out alive, wouldn't you think?

There's a simple answer to these questions. In many cases, the police and government officials are not only inept, but also corrupt. If it weren't so sad, it would be almost comical to read some of the stories about the police involvement. For example, earlier in 1998, the top law-enforcement group in Mexico established an elite anti-kidnapping unit aimed at combating the rising problem and escalating violence in these types of cases. That elite group was withdrawn after three of its members were arrested the following May for guess what—KIDNAPPING!

Chihuahua State Police arrested three members of another such unit after relatives of a kidnapped woman paid a ransom to a man who was later identified as a federal policeman. The statement handed down from the federal attorney's office said its investigations found that these men had committed several illicit acts.

Government and military involvement in these criminal activities have, unfortunately, positioned all officials as criminals in the minds of foreign travelers, which causes an air of distrust and chaos in Mexico. Fewer and fewer tourists now venture into Mexico and spend less and less money. This hurts the Mexican economy, which in turn creates more crime due to the economic struggles of its people. It's a vicious cycle, and officials and police chiefs are resigning from office, thus causing their "so-called" justice system to spin out of control. Worst of all, there appears to be little to no help on the horizon.

What a shame for the millions of honest, hard-working Mexican citizens whose businesses and families suffer because of the *desperados* who make great copy for international press. Mexico is an incredibly beautiful country with crystal, aquamarine waters and sparkling white sands that beckon to the adventurous visitor or the progressive businessman. For visitors, the country holds a fascination with ancient ruins and unparalleled beaches. The people, as a whole, are eager to please their visitors, and bargain seekers can find it a virtual treasure chest of great opportunities to purchase and ship back home a little piece of Mexican culture. The promise of corporate prosperity is equally as great, as evidenced by many international firms now doing a tremendous amount of business in Mexico. It's the element of crime and desperation that reveal the ugly side of this beautiful country, and its ugly side is threatening to break the back of Mexico's struggling economy.

Now that you know the truth of the matter, will you ever visit Mexico again? Will you make a decision to expand your business inside its borders? I certainly hope so! If not, you'll be missing a ton of excitement and perhaps even some prosperous business opportunities. The trick is to become aware of the possibilities and let your better judgment rule.

This book was written to make you more aware, not to create so much fear that you refuse to experience the wonders of Mexico. I wouldn't feel right about leaving you with this chapter full of all the problems yet offering you no solutions. Even though the last chapter offers you a menu of solutions to common challenges faced by vacationers and corporate travelers, it by no means is all you'll need to know if you frequently cross Mexico's borders. It's a start, and I'm obligated and privileged to offer you a touch of the information you'll need to have. However, if your stay is extended in time or distance to the interior of Mexico, or if your corporation is expanding its operations to include the many opportunities Mexico has to offer new businesses, you'll want to order my catalogue of services and products. I'll be your personal guide to Mexico. I can promise you, the price you pay in these products and/or services will be much less expensive than what you or your company could pay if you were kidnapped.

CHAPTER SEVENTEEN
Preventative Action

Although kidnapping is what I have first-hand experience of, it by no means makes up the majority of violent crimes in Mexico. God forbid you ever face the problems I had to, or that you fall victim to any criminal activity in Mexico. But like motorcycle riding without a helmet in a major U.S. city, it's probably just a matter of time before you become another statistic. Think of this last chapter as a type of helmet for crossing the borders of Mexico.

The following information is in no special order of importance or frequency of occurrence, it's just meant to be a directory of preventative suggestions and tips on how to avoid becoming the latest reported crime statistic—that's no way to make headlines, right? Even though these tips are specific to traveling in Mexico, many could also be applied to any foreign country and any critical situation outside the United States. So, pick those that fit your present needs. Share the information you read between these pages with a friend who might remember just one thing you told them that could save his or her life in an emergency. Wouldn't that be a reward to know what you said saved the life of another? It doesn't get much better than that—why, you'd be more listened to than E. F. Hutton!

The following have been developed from personal experience, experiences others have shared with me, and those my development team have researched while putting together our preventative travel tips for our informational manual. For further travel suggestions, or should you have any questions about other products in our Stand International Catalog of products and services, don't hesitate to look on the back page of this book. Within days of contacting Stand International, you'll receive our immediate attention and response to your concerns.

Preventative Action Tips while Traveling in Mexico

✧ Always read travel warnings. If you are a
  U.S.citizen, these are issued by the State
  Department based on all relevant information
  about traveling to certain desirable and
  undesirable destinations.

✧ Look up the consular information sheets. These
  are available for every country in the world. They
  will tell you where to find the U.S. Embassy or
  Consulate for that particular country, including
  those in Mexico. Within these sheets, you will also
  discover any health conditions or minor political
  problems not covered in the news. Also included
  are unusual currency and entry regulations, crime
  and security information and drug penalties.

✧ Know the current entry requirements. As of this printing, proof of citizenship and photo identification (such as your driver's license) are all that are needed for entry into Mexico. However, if your stay extends past 180 days or goes deeper into the country, these requirements are subject to change.

✧ Know the amount of goods you may bring into the country. Currently, you may only "walk in" with $50 worth of goods. Anything over that will be taxed at 32.8 percent.

✧ Avoid taking a taxi not summoned by telephone or by a friend in the country. Decline random offers at the airport to take you to your hotel. Taxicab crime is rampant in Mexico. Passengers are picked up, robbed, beaten and left for dead. Refuse to become a victim to these daily occurrences.

✧ Leave valuables and irreplaceable items in a safe place—like home!

✧ Avoid wearing expensive jewelry or designer clothing, and carry only the cash or credit cards you'll be needing for that outing. Large amounts of cash will not only make you a target, but might also bring you under suspicion for money laundering by local officials. It's also a good idea to bring traveler's checks with you instead of large amounts of cash.

Terror In Mexico:
The Kidnapping of Ken Krusensterna

 ✧ The areas behind the U.S. Embassy and the Zona Rosa, a restaurant/shopping area near the Embassy, are the highest crime zones against U.S. citizens. Use caution if you must be in or around this area.

 ✧ Do not hitchhike or accept rides from strangers.

 ✧ Make sure that any bus travel you might do is done during daylight hours and on first-class conveyances.

 ✧ Avoid using ATM cards and machines in Mexico. If one must be used, do so only during the business day at large, protected facilities.

 ✧ Be careful when ordering beverages in local nightclubs and bars, especially in the evening. Some establishments may contaminate or drug the drinks to gain control over the patron.

 ✧ Exercise caution when traveling all highways in Mexico. Reported highway incidents include robbery, kidnapping and murder.

 ✧ The State of Chiapas is an extremely volatile location. The Mexican military has reestablished authority there, but there is still an armed rebel presence in the more remote areas of the state. This area is considered to be highly unstable.

✧ The state of Ciudad Juarez has become the focal point for narcotics smuggling in the past few years. Many U.S. citizens have been murdered; others have been kidnapped and hundreds imprisoned after involving themselves in drugs in Mexico. Know the drug penalties, or better yet, just avoid the situations altogether.

✧ Sentences for drug penalties in Mexico can be as long as 25 years plus fines. And, Mexican prisons make ours in the U.S. look like country clubs. The purchase of controlled medication requires a doctor's prescription. Even with this knowledge, Mexico keeps its drug laws very vague. If you must purchase medicine there, make certain to check with the nearest Mexican consulate beforehand.

✧ Penalties for firearms can carry sentences ranging from 5-30 years for a non-assault weapon. You must obtain a permit. Some sections of Mexico do not allow the possession of knives or anything that might be construed as a weapon.

✧ Do not offer rides to strangers, especially when approaching a border! Harboring aliens is a serious felony under both U.S. and Mexican law.

✧ Adequate medical care can be found in all major cities; however, if you are in the more remote areas, it may be limited. Also, payment for services rendered is often due before release. Check with your medical insurer to make certain that you are covered in Mexico, and ask how to go about obtaining supplemental insurance if you are not.

✧ Your driver's license is valid in Mexico, however, most often your insurance is not. You should obtain full coverage when driving in Mexico. If you do decide to drive in Mexico, be extra cautious at night. Livestock roam freely about, and in the dark it is hard to see a Black Angus bull until it's too late. Also, an oncoming vehicle flashing its lights is a warning for you to slow down or pull over because you are approaching a narrow bridge. The first vehicle to flash customarily has the right of way in these situations.

✧ There is definitely something to the old adage, "Don't Drink the Water." It has been a common problem in Mexico for decades. It would be much safer for you to purchase bottled water from one of the many distributors. There are as many bottled water companies as there are taxicabs; the bottled water is a lot safer, though!

✧ If you cannot handle spicy foods, be careful. Even the more subtle foods can mask some hidden kicks!

✧ If you are staying at a hotel, never invite strangers to your room. Keep your room keys well protected and out of sight. Never forget to deadbolt your room before leaving and put the chain on at night while sleeping.

✦ Make certain that your family knows your itinerary. It's a good idea to let them know that you will check in with them each night. Don't alter your plans. I can tell you what a pain in the ass that can be!

✦ Don't forget about the deadly effects of the sun. Mexico is closer to the equator, and those of you who are not from a bordering southwestern town may have some real problems adjusting.

✦ Know some helpful phrases in Spanish. This will not only make your trip more convenient but also help you to appear less vulnerable and more prepared.

✦ Keep a copy of your passport in a different location from the original. If your passport should happen to get lost or stolen, the copy can expedite the process to obtain a new one.

✦ If you happen to be traveling to some of the more remote areas of Mexico, remember that malaria is still present in many of their villages. See your doctor before you leave home and take the recommended dosage of chloroquine.

Terror In Mexico:
The Kidnapping of Ken Krusensterna

✧ The altitude of Mexico City is very high. Some people may be susceptible to problems associated with higher altitudes.

✧ Keep in mind that pickpockets and robbers come in all shapes and sizes. Small children and women are just as likely to be involved in petty theft as a shifty looking man.

✧ When participating in various recreational activities, there's also a few things to be aware of:
1. Sports and aquatic equipment that you rent may not be up to the standards we expect in the U.S. Make sure to thoroughly check out the rental place.
2. Several tourists have been killed in jet-ski accidents when inexperienced tour guides allow their clients to follow too closely or to operate the ski unsafely.
3. When para-sailing, more often than not, by signing your name on a passenger list, you are relieving the company of any liability for your safety.
4. Do not use pools or beaches without lifeguards. Always remember that in the U.S., we have very high standards for safety. That is not always the case with foreign countries.
5. When diving, do not dive into bodies of water in which you are not familiar. Mexican waters are notorious for hidden rock formations.

Finally, if you find yourself in trouble in Mexico, for any reason, contact the U.S. Embassy. Looking up the number after the fact may be impossible, so be sure to have a copy of all necessary numbers and contact's names and addresses to take with you. Leave behind a copy of all your contacts, numbers, embassy information and any other numbers a family member may need to have in order to reach you in case of an emergency. One statistic that you'll want to keep in mind is that Mexico has the highest number of arrests of Americans abroad over 1,000 per year. It's big business in Mexico—much like kidnapping, only a tad more legal!

Most of all, prepare properly for traveling in a foreign country—especially Mexico. When you do, you'll be protected by the armor of knowledge and clothed in the confidence of wisdom.

CHAPTER EIGHTEEN
Time To Take A Stand

I've formed a new company since recovering from my experience in Mexico because it just wasn't acceptable for me to give the bastards any more of my life. They had 12 whole days of control over my physical body and sometimes even over my thoughts, but I wasn't about to give them any more than that. That's how Stand International, Inc. was born. It was born from sheer stubbornness, a determination that I was going to take a stand and fight for my rights and the rights of others traveling in Mexico.

You know; there is a lot to be said for anger. You can let it eat you up inside, or you can use it to move you toward your life's purpose—and, that was my choice. I really believe I beat the odds; there was a reason why I survived when many others have not. Perhaps it was because I was mentally or physically stronger than most—well, perhaps. Or, maybe it was because I'm just too mean and the good die young. How I survived the ordeal really isn't the most important thing. It's more a question of why I survived. If there is a reason for me to have experienced this and lived to tell my story, then I have to believe others, like you, needed to hear it.

Chapter Eighteen:
Time To Take A Stand

Imagine with me if you will that there are absolutely no coincidences in life—that what happens to us is by our own design, and our experiences are the consequences of our own decisions. If this is truth, then I could have and should have taken steps to prevent what happened to me. If a little knowledge and a lot more common sense could have prevented me from becoming a victim, it could do the same for you too. At this day in time, most of us are no strangers to violent crimes and random terrorism right in our own cities. But, we've learned what to do; we've been taught by our past experiences that there are certain things we can do to stay out of harms way. Why is it when many visit Mexico, even if it's for a vacation getaway, that common sense and awareness takes a vacation as well?

I'm not usually a "why me" kind of thinker, especially if it puts me in that whinny, negative position. However, for the first few weeks after the kidnapping, I questioned "Why me?" Why is it my family had to go through this? Why is it I have to live with the fear and aftermath of surviving such a life-altering experience? Well, nobody wants to be around a whiner, including the whiner himself, so I gave up the pity party and went to work to really discover the purpose for the pain. I took a stand!

What came out of it all was Stand International. Now I'm not the only one taking a stand against terrorism and violent crime across the border. Everybody attending my seminars leaves the room better equipped to protect themselves, their families, their friends and business associates and even their personal and professional property. Stand International has created a shield of protective awareness that can be carried by all those in the know. Knowledge is a wonderful thing, but it has to be shared and acted upon in order to make it a powerful tool.

I now travel all over the country teaching corporations how to protect their employees traveling in Mexico. Every time I'm in a group of people who know about my experience, I find myself fielding questions and giving some advice on how to become more aware of the dangers of traveling across the border. I've appeared on numerous radio and television programs to share my story with curious listeners, and perhaps even been the topic of conversation around their dinner tables after hearing snippets of my story on a nightly news program. All those things have been an incredible experience, and I can honestly say I've enjoyed every minute, but when the hoopla dies down what's to be learned?

Although Stand International has been a profitable business for me, it's not about turning a buck. I have a different perspective on business since my kidnapping. I used to love getting paid for creating great business. Now I have created a great business that I love—and, I get paid. See the difference? When I had my trucking business, ran a hotel, and throughout the years when I've invested in different companies, my focus was profit—how can I get the most bang for my buck. I made good profit in almost every venture because of the people who helped me in those organizations. I've changed my working philosophy these days. The focus of Stand International is to help people, and in doing so Stand International continues to be a success.

So, exactly what do we do at Stand International? First, I did what I always do when I form a new business, I surrounded myself with a team of professionals. With me I have gathered those who research, write, design and develop materials that are made available to both corporations and individuals who want to learn how to be safe in Mexico. Stand International can make these materials available to you and your company. What I most enjoy is learning about your company and its needs and forming workshops to meet your specifications. Then I can speak to your people about company specific issues and offer them suggestions and ideas that make their travels safe and productive. When I speak to your people, I also make available materials that help managers and executives support and coach the employees that frequently travel to Mexico. Our materials are not just a bunch of fluff, offering you a tip or two about what to do to protect yourself. Instead, our travel manual offers the latest in Mexican law and regulations, travel warnings, preventative measures, crisis planning, packing your protective needs, potential danger awareness, money exchanges, and adopting a foreigner's mindset. It also offers all the numbers and contacts your family, business associates and you will need in case the unexpected happens and you're caught in a crisis across the border.

Without awareness and knowledge, without preparation and a changed perspective, the potential dangers of traveling into Mexico are ten-fold. Recognizing a dangerous situation is the first step in being able to avoid it. It's much easier for the criminal to fool the foolish, and much easier for the targeted victim to foil the plan when they expect and plan for the unexpected. Victims are chosen by their victimizing behavior, and even a little bit of knowledge gives you the confidence and mindset that can make the hunter search another prey.

By listening to and learning the message of Stand International, together we'll be sending a message to Mexican desperadoes—CRIME DOESN'T PAY. When they learn that our corporate funds won't be lining their pockets, they'll take another look at their chosen occupations, and you'll return home in safety. If the exchange of business ideas and innovation is to continue to take place between Mexico and the U. S., we've all got to improve the way business is conducted. Stand International is one of the answers to that concern.

Our Mexican corporate counterparts are also participating in the need to keep the flow of foreign dollars filtering into their organizations by doing their part to support and inform business travelers. Stand International keeps in close contact with managers and workers of Mexican corporations that are currently doing business with the U.S. Our constant communications with them have given us a tremendous advantage in being able to offer you and your company the latest news. We are informed of the "hot" areas where bands of violent criminals have formed, told of the newest types of crimes being practiced on the unsuspecting travelers, and advised of the best ways to prevent or cope with a crisis.

Stand International is all about partnerships, really. We have formed partnerships with the top U. S. corporations who are currently doing business in Mexico and helped them to keep their employees and products safe. We have formed partnerships with the Mexican corporations and, in turn, have helped them to secure a constant flow of profitable business free of the long-term damage that fear creates. We have helped corporate executives to form partnerships with their employees' families in order for them to feel more confident about their loved ones traveling to Mexico. And, we are now forming partnerships with officials on both sides of the border so that our programs offer today's solutions for tomorrow's challenges.

We at Stand International have found that an early investment in time and funds that help to keep your people safe, will certainly provide great returns. In our litigious society, can you imagine what would happen if a manager was kidnapped or murdered because the company failed to practice proper intervention methods and offer ongoing educational opportunities? While it's certainly not possible or economically feasible for companies to put all their employees traveling in Mexico in bullet-proof vests and transport them in armored cars, it is necessary to increase their awareness and give them the tools they'll need for additional personal protection. That's the job of Stand International.

Corporate travelers, of course, aren't the only ones in danger of becoming the victims of violent crimes. What if you're the occasional vacationer? It's common for students on spring break to plan a getaway to Rocky Point, or newlyweds to take a honeymoon to Cancun. The materials Stand International offers can help you know what paperwork you'll need and how to properly prepare so that a one- or two-week vacation doesn't turn into a lifetime of hurt. For the

Terror In Mexico:
The Kidnapping of Ken Krusensterna

vacationer, we offer smaller pamphlets that are easy and convenient to pack in your tote, and a copy can be left with the family as well. They can be broken down by the city, region or town you're planning to visit.

There is no excuse for you to enter Mexico unprepared, but that still may not guarantee that danger won't cross your path. That's why we've included our well-thought-out crisis plan. Your company, family, friends and you should know what to do to help you survive a crisis. I always go back to the information that was given to my son during my ordeal. "No *policia* . . . no *policia*." Let me tell you, if Keith hadn't of had the courage to go with his gut, I doubt whether I'd be here today. He called the police and when he couldn't get the locals to act quickly, he called in the F.B.I. I'm not saying that is the answer in every situation, and I cannot recommend one way over another, but I can offer the contacts and numbers on both sides of the border you'll need so that you'll have them at your fingertips. Precious time lost could mean your loved one's life.

Give our people at Stand International a call, or contact us by mail or fax and we'll be happy to analyze your needs, help you discover the best way to satisfy those needs, and prepare you for safe vacations and business opportunities in Mexico. This is not a circumstance where ignorance is bliss—it could be a killer. Why jeopardize yourself or your employees when safety could be only a phone call away?

One favor I ask of you; it helps us to monitor our information and workshops. Let our people at Stand International know what you thought of the materials and information provided, and how you might be better served. It's your frontline stories that feed us with the insight and first-hand knowledge that keeps us at the cutting edge of personal protection. It's your experiences that help us to save others from suffering similar heartaches. I can't tell you how many horror stories I've heard where the "IF ONLY" message was echoed throughout its telling. "If only I'd known I couldn't have ammunition in my car—I had no guns so I thought the box of shells was harmless." Or, "If only I'd told my family that I changed hotels—they would have known where to begin the search." Even, "If only I'd listened to that warning voice in my head—I would have taken the necessary steps to better prepare and plan for my trip into Mexico." Those "IF ONLY" speeches can break your heart and cripple your company.

So, after all my warnings, I can assure you, it is possible to have a wonderful experience vacationing and doing business in Mexico. Just be aware—don't be blind to the possibilities—all the possibilities. If you let your enjoyment override your common sense, your pleasure in Mexico could be short-lived. Keep your antennas up, your warning lights on. Learn to categorize your perceived warning signals. If you see something that could create a snag in your travels, prepare for those anticipated moments and give it a green light. If you observe something in Mexico that makes you question or take a second look, inform your hotel manager or traveling company and companions and give it a yellow "proceed with caution" light. If you see or hear something that makes the hairs on the back of your neck and arms stand up, give it a "red" light—put the brakes on and get the heck out of there. There's a time for right—a time for

Terror In Mexico:
The Kidnapping of Ken Krusensterna

fight—and a time for flight. Educate yourself and learn when to do what. Education and knowledge is always useful, often preventative, and sometimes even life sustaining. Remember; the time you saved by _not_ attending a personal safety workshop could be the first few hours of a lifetime spent regretting your absence!

Epilogue

I've always heard never to pray for patience because you'll be opening up Pandora's box. Although I don't remember praying for patience, I do listen to that inner voice of warning and have a bit of a spiritual side to me that is my positive advisor, my teacher and my guide through life. I am also a believer that things happen for a reason, and that is how my new company STAND INTERNATIONAL, INC. was formed—to help international travelers become more aware and in control while visiting a foreign country, especially Mexico. I've been told that I'm a statistical miracle, but I know that my survival and current business ventures have all been part of a larger master plan.

If this book has entertained you—great! If it has made you aware that you need to do your homework when traveling into Mexico—even better! Now I pass the baton to you, and give you the responsibility to pass along the story to others like yourself who may be planning an international trip or doing frequent business in Mexico. Knowledge alone can change nothing, but knowledge with action can change the world. One person—YOU—might make all the difference in the lives of those you work and live with if you share my story. Like I said, I certainly don't wish to repeat this lesson, and because of what I've experienced and learned, I hope to save you from a similar fate.

I look forward to the opportunities this experience has allowed me, and one of those might be to meet you in person at a corporate international security seminar or while I'm on tour to promote this book. If we do have a chance to meet, I believe it won't be by chance but by design. There is one thing I've learned during this experience, and that is that things do not happen by chance or coincidence, and it was no coincidence that I lived to tell my story. It too will be no coincidence if we meet and exchange stories or ideas.

If you work for a corporation or organization that travels to Mexico, it is paramount that they do everything possible to prepare themselves and their people to meet and overcome the challenges presented by international travel. Let them know my story and perhaps I can provide some answers to their personal security questions before they open themselves up to similar dangers. There is no need for anyone to be ignorant of how to protect themselves and their property. It is my goal for everybody's experience of international travel to be a positive one.

If you have a unique story to share or a suggestion on how to protect yourself when traveling internationally that could benefit others, please contact me at . . .

> Ken Krusensterna, President
> Stand International
> 515 E. Carefree Hwy.,   Suite 151
> Phoenix, AZ   85085
> Off: 623-434-1709
> Fax: 623-516-8184

Order Form

Book* - Terror in Mexico: The Kidnapping of Ken Krusensterna
   Regular Price: $19.95   **Pre-order Price: $17.95**

Manual*
   Regular Price: $74.95   **Pre-order Price: $69.95**

Book & Manual Package
   Regular Price: $94.90   **Pre-order Price: $87.90**

*Projected Delivery Date: January 2000
Please inquire about additional Corporate Discounts

Please Ship Me:

___ **Books @ $17.95 ea.**	Total Purchase Amount: $ _____
___ **Manuals @ $69.95 ea.**	+ 6.8% Sales Tax: (AZ Only): $ _____
___ **Packages @ $87.90 ea.**	**Total Order Amount: $ _____**

Make Checks Payable to **Stand International**

Name: _____

Title: _____

Company: _____

Address: _____

City: _____   State: _____   Zip: _____

Phone: (___) _____   Fax: (___) _____